Bread and Butter
BASKETBALL

Bread and Butter
BASKETBALL

ALVIN F. "DOGGIE" JULIAN

Basketball Coach
Dartmouth College

PRENTICE-HALL, INC., Englewood Cliffs, N.J.

PRINTED IN THE UNITED STATES OF AMERICA

08146—BC

To my sons

ALVIN AND TOBY

ACKNOWLEDGMENTS

I want to acknowledge with a great deal of gratitude and appreciation my basketball association with BIRNEY CRUM, Muhlenberg coach. Birney taught me a great part of my basketball and I owe a great deal to him.

And to CLAIR BEE, a long time friend and counselor. Clair has been invaluable in his aid to me in basketball. He is one of the great men in the game and I am deeply indebted to him.

And to WALTER BROWN of the Boston Garden. When I came to New England, Walter made things easier for me. And, when I coached the Boston Celtics, he was without doubt the greatest boss in the world. He has been a great help and a real friend.

To HOLY CROSS COLLEGE where I received the finest possible treatment. I could never thank this fine college enough.

And last but not least, to the many great athletes who have played for me down through the years. Through their efforts I have been able to write this book. They were loyal and faithful in dark times and I can never thank them enough.

"Doggie" Julian's Game . . .

The game of basketball has changed considerably in the last few years. And the author, having been in the game for many years, has not stood still. He has progressed with the game.

Certain phases of basketball, however, will always be a part of the game and Doggie Julian calls these phases the "bread and butter" aspects of the game. Doggie's bread and butter approach to basketball makes sound reading for coaches, players and for the fans. It is good reading from start to finish and the illustrations add spice to the narrative.

Coach Julian's book reminds one and all that the frills of the game are all right but that fundamentals are the proof of the pudding. Doggie hits and hits hard on these fundamentals and the reader of this book will soon realize that much of his success has been the result of his devotion to the basic factors of the game. No approach and no aspect of the game for the player, the coach, or the fan is overlooked.

Along with the basic fundamentals and the "Simon Legree" drills, Doggie Julian also includes bench strategy, locker room procedure, and opponent scouting. Included in the book are actual scouting reports used by Coach Julian in his work at Dartmouth where his team has won the Ivy League title in three of the past four years. These reports are done in the style which Julian first utilized in taking Muhlenberg to the National Invitational Championship in 1944 and in 1945 and at Holy Cross when his team won the NCAA title in 1947–1948. These reports include personnel evaluation, individual skills, team play, and shot charts.

No player, coach, or fan should miss this book. It is chock full of pertinent, homey, down-to-earth, bread and butter basketball. That's Doggie Julian's game!

RONALD W. "DUDLEY" MOORE
La Salle College
Philadelphia, Penna.

vii

This Game of Basketball

I coach basketball because I like to eat, my family likes to eat, my friends like to eat, and I know the only way I can keep the whole gang eating is to win some games. If you and your gang don't like bread and butter in your diet—don't read any further—put this book down and go eat your cake.

So many basketball books and treatises have been published concerning fundamentals, skills, and techniques that this book would only be another for the collector's shelf if I followed the usual pattern. So—I have written this one from the point of view of applied coaching—down-to-earth, bread and butter basketball which the players must apply on the court.

The language presented here is the only basketball language I know. It represents the words and phrases and basketball terminology which I use in my everyday teaching and coaching of the game. "How much rice can a Chinaman eat?" "French Pastry!" "Scrambled eggs!" What have these to do with *Bread and Butter Basketball?* That's what I hope to bring out in this book.

Even in today's run-and-shoot basketball there are certain bread and butter fundamentals which will always be an important part of coaching and playing.

The "26 Rules" found in this book cover, in a great measure, principles and philosophies which can be applied to any player or team regardless of the size of the players or the type of offense or defense used. I have tried to explain what is meant when we use these rules. Let's take Number 1 for instance: "The ball is 20 karat gold!" No one throws gold away; and a good basketball player does not throw the ball away. You must have the ball to win! Why give it away?

I believe that humor has its place in sports and in coaching. If a player does not get some fun out of the game—he shouldn't play. Coach and player can have fun and still win. In fact, I think fun and winning go hand in hand. If coaching and playing are like pulling teeth you and your players had better get some needles and yarn and take up knitting.

Another thing. A lot of us round-ball experts get to thinking that basketball is the only game in the world and that the world is worse for having any other game. This kind of thinking narrows our teaching and is for the birds.

I think one of the greatest contributions to winning is the willingness of the players to pool their personalities into one being—the team! Today, the high scorers get all the publicity while the boy who plays a great defensive game, who handicaps the opponents' high scorer, receives little attention. This is frequently true of the rebounder, too—the guy who gets you that apple all the time. The willingness of these self-sacrificing players to scorn praise and to step backstage and let the spotlight fall on the basket-makers is what makes the great team.

What makes the difference in who gets the credit? As far as I am concerned they can give the bus driver the credit—just so we win! The team must be successful or the star is unimportant. The fans always remember *every* player on a championship or winning team but they seldom remember any player on a losing team.

I never did believe that coaches were magicians. But I do believe that a good coach can help good players and that a poor coach will handicap any player. Most coaches know their business or they wouldn't be in it and when you have the horses you'll win. "Players make coaches! Coaches don't make players!" If a player hasn't got speed, how are you going to give it to him? Only God can do that. If a boy is a poor shooter, you may improve him a little but you'll never make him a great scorer. Another thing. You don't play with "ifs." You play with what you've got! Why say: "If I only had the big man. . . ." You don't have him so you have to play without him. If you start "iffing" too much you become a dreamer and not a coach.

I want speed and courage in a player. But too often I get the "half-baked potato who isn't good enough to eat but not bad enough to throw away." The fortunes of this game change swiftly. You who have been coaching a long time know that basketball is like a wagon wheel that goes around and around. "Now it's on the top and now it's on the bottom." For those of you who have not been in the game very long or are just starting—you'll soon find that every dog has his day and that all you have to do is to keep working and hustling and it may be your turn to be on top the next time around.

Let me conclude this introduction with a story. Little Johnny, eight years old, came home one night and started bombing his dad with questions. This particular night his dad was tired and wanted to put on his slippers and rest. But little Johnny persisted. Finally, his dad went over to the bookcase and got a map of the world. He tore the map into small pieces, got some scotch tape, and said: "Here, Johnny! Take this map of the world and put it together. When you are finished I will answer all the questions you want."

The father thought this was good for a couple of hours, but, to his amazement, Johnny was back in twenty minutes with the map of the world put together perfectly. Every country and continent was right where it belonged. The father said: "Why, Johnny, how did you do it?" Shaking his head in amazement, he continued: "Why, son, I should be asking you questions!"

Little Johnny smiled and replied: "It was easy, Dad. Look!" He held the map up to his father and then turned it slowly to the other side. "You see, Dad, on the other side is the picture of a little boy. If you put that boy together right, the world will be all right."

I hope all of you are proud to belong to a profession that is trying to put boys together right. As long as we keep trying to do that there will always be bread and butter on the table.

ALVIN F. "DOGGIE" JULIAN

Table of Contents

Chapter 10: DARTMOUTH'S MAN-TO-MAN DEFENSE *(Cont.)*

Opponent; Switching. Defensing the Big Man: Screen Big Man from Ball; In front, three-quarters or half-way; Defensing high pivot or high fast; Call the play; Guarding Positions; A Team Job; Clair Bee's One-Three-One Zone; The Three-Two Zone.

Zone Defense. Usage; Zone Strength and Weakness; Adjustments; Fast Break. Two-One-Two Zone: Positions and Moves; Territory Limitations; High Post and Inside Pivot Defense Positions. The Dartmouth One-Two-Two Zone: Shot Charts; Positions and Moves. Zone the Big Man: One-Three-One; Positions and Moves. Two-Three: Positions and Moves.

Man-to-Man Defense Variations: Man-to-Man Press Positions and Moves; Two-Two-One Press Positions and Moves; Zone Press Positions and Moves; One-Two-One-One Press Positions and Moves. Combination Defenses. Defensive Drills: Front, Slide, Switch; One-on-One; One-on-Two; Two-on-Two; Blocking-Out; Switch on Ball; Defensive Shuttle; Zone Defense Drills; Screen-Switch Drill.

Pre-Season Organization and Plans; Player Information; Managers' Duties and Responsibilities; The Trainer; Pre-Season Conditioning; Drills; Half-Court Practice; Full-Court Practice; Scrimmages; Team Selection; Substitutions; Having Fun; Dressing Room; Player relations; Injuries; Get Tough; Speed; Defense.

Offensive Fundamentals and Techniques; Offensive and Defensive Check Lists; Warm-Up; Passing; Shooting; Screens and Shots. One-on-Two Defensive Drill; Switching Drill; Jump Ball Drill. Basic Plays Drill; Defensive Fundamentals and Techniques. Fast Break and Shuttle Drill. Half Court Practice.

Shooting; Fast Break; System Skeleton Plays; Give-and-Go; Swinging the Pivot; Clear-Outs; Half-Court Offense; Blocking-Out and Offensive and Defensive Rebounding; Full Court Scrimmage; Offensive and Defensive Fundamentals: Offensive Block-Off; "Crotch" and "Switch"; Skeleton Plays; Rebound and Fast Break Drill.

Bread and Butter
BASKETBALL

KEY TO DIAGRAMS

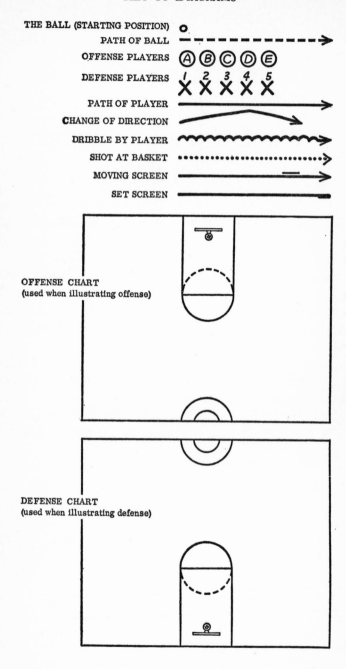

THE BALL (STARTING POSITION)

PATH OF BALL

OFFENSE PLAYERS

DEFENSE PLAYERS

PATH OF PLAYER

CHANGE OF DIRECTION

DRIBBLE BY PLAYER

SHOT AT BASKET

MOVING SCREEN

SET SCREEN

OFFENSE CHART
(used when illustrating offense)

DEFENSE CHART
(used when illustrating defense)

Introduction

The 26 Magic Numbers

I realize that some of these rules overlap but they are simple to remember and will help to impress the principles upon your players. Your players will get to know them and often inject a little fun into the practices by repeating one of these rules to a teammate who has made a mistake. We get a great kick out of them and find them very helpful. Fundamentally, we think they are sound, simple to teach, easy to remember, and will apply to any style of play or any group of players regardless of age.

Chuck Kaufman, a Dartmouth captain, once asked why I didn't say the ball was 24-karat gold. He said: "You know, coach, the higher the karat, the more valuable the gold." I said: "Sure, Chuck, I know. But the higher the karat in gold, the softer it is. We don't want our basketball to be too soft."

1. *The ball! It's 20-karat gold. . . .*

"Too many players and teams are careless with the ball!" Hang on to the leather! It's 20-karat gold! All too often a team will get the ball through an interception or a loose ball and lose it right back again because of a poor or thoughtless pass. Make haste slowly and be determined to hold on to the ball until you or one of your teammates gets a good shot. Bad passes and poor shots are the stock-in-trade of a poor team.

2. *Be careful on a lay-up! It's money in the bank. . . .*

"More games are won on lay-up shots than on any other!"

And more games are lost because of bad lay-up shots than by any other shot. The lay-up is the most important shot in basketball but it is often missed because the shooter wants to be fancy or because he doesn't slow down before releasing the ball. It is better for the shooter to slow down after the drive and make the lay-up soft and easy than to *look good* on the drive and *miss* the shot. All players should learn to shoot with the left hand on the left side of the basket and with the right hand on the right side of the basket. Then, they won't have to cross the backboard to shoot and their opponents can't concentrate on their favorite hands. Shooters should cut on an angle toward the basket, never in a semi-circle.

3. *Basketball is a game of motion! It's your move.* . . . .

"Motion on the court is vital!" Many players stand still and "ball beg." This kind of a player seems to think the ball should be passed to him in any situation. When he doesn't get the ball, he usually just stands there looking and watching the game. He should have a chair! In the balcony! When a teammate passes to a good player, he gets out of there and takes his opponent with him. This move opens up the court for someone else. All teams hate to play against opponents who keep the ball hopping and MOVE.

4. *Always fake direction! Remember "Wrong Way" Corrigan.* . . . .

"Faking is important because it tricks opponents into making mistakes!" However, the good faker gives his opponent a chance to be faked and does not attempt to fake a "dumb" ballplayer. The dumb ballplayer won't react. The smart one will! The faker should also frequently "go" the way he has just faked. Then again, the good faker doesn't fake too much. . . . He will often go without faking.

5. *Move to beat the pass! Be where you ain't.* . . . .

"Beating and meeting the pass is the stamp of a good ballplayer!" The player who moves and cuts and meets the ball makes it duck soup for a teammate to pass to him. Such action also keeps his opponent so busy that he can't find time to attempt to steal the ball. Hand in hand with beating and meeting the pass goes the fake to receive or meet the ball and the reverse cut (particularly when the defensive player is over-shifting). When a player moves to meet or beat the pass he should make sure he is in position to catch the ball; to return the pass and cut; to feed another cutter or the pivot; and to shoot.

6. *When in trouble make a V! "V" for Victory. . . .*

"A player in the wrong position can get right by making a 'V!' " A player never goes wrong when he feels he is in the wrong position if he makes a V, because he "clears out" and he takes his opponent with him. This is an important fundamental and is particularly good when more than one player cuts at the same time. However, a player should *never* "V" toward the basket.

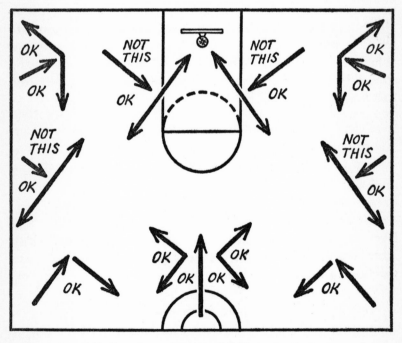

DIAGRAM 1. *"V" Situations.* Players should instinctively recognize the correct "V" to make in the above positions on the floor.

7. Don't think for the opponents! Be yourself. . . .

"Some players are more concerned with what they think the opponents are thinking than with what they are thinking for themselves!" Frequently, when you ask a player why he did not go through with a cut or a play he will say: "Well, Coach, the defense was going to do this or that. . . ." How does he or anyone else *know* what a defensive player or team is going to do? The player should go through with his move and if the opponent or opponents play him right, he hasn't lost anything. If the opponent or opponents play him wrong, he has accomplished something. By thinking for the defense, the player has helped the opponents play their defense well, and he has also hurt his own team by a bad move and one which his teammates did not expect.

8. One player cuts at a time! Stay out of the act. . . .

"If a teammate is cutting and you are in his way, 'V' out of the play!" When a player starts a cut and sees that a teammate is also cutting, he should make a V. All players should remember: Only one cutter at a time! The good player realizes that two cutters will bring their defensive men where they will be in good position to "double-team" the ball or stop the play. Further, two cutters often jam things up and they frequently run into one another. The good player keeps cutting even if he does not get the ball and he realizes the vital importance of timing to his team's offense.

9. Grab it! Don't tap it. . . .

"Too often a player makes the mistake of tapping the ball under the defensive basket." This is bad because the ball often goes out of bounds and becomes the opponent's ball. Too, the tapper often taps the ball into the hands of an opponent and, not infrequently, into the opponent's basket. The good rebounder doesn't stab at the ball . . . he grabs it! Under the offensive basket it is all right to tap the ball back up but, even here, a player is better off if he can grab the ball and then go back up with it for the shot. If he is in a poor position or is closely pressed, a deep back tap to his teammates in the back court is permissible.

10. *Never force a shot! Look before you leap.* . . .

"THE OPPONENTS WILL NEVER BLOCK A *GOOD SHOT!*" A shot should never be blocked if it is attempted at the right time. A team should be sure it has rebound strength under the basket before a shot is attempted. Good offensive and defensive balance is important and all offensive players should be sure their opponents are not forcing them to shoot unnaturally (bad arch on ball; shooting from a spot too far away; attempting shots they seldom practice). If the defensive man has been successful in making it tough for a player to get a shot away, he should pass off to a teammate and MOVE. He will get his shot sooner or later. If a player's shot is blocked, he shouldn't have shot. A player should never shoot when well guarded by a defensive opponent (forcing the shot). He should fake a shot occasionally and drive or follow a fake with the shot. When under the basket, a fake lay-up followed by the actual shot is usually successful (particularly when an opponent is breathing down the shooter's neck). All players should take their best shots when the chips are down. All too frequently, a player will take his poorest shot at a crucial moment and, unaccountably, often take a shot he doesn't even practice. Don't ask me why! It's one of the mysteries. . . .

DIAGRAM 2. *Bouncing the Ball!* A passes to B and goes behind and receives a return pass. Under no conditions should A now bounce the ball because he will have limited himself to a pass or a shot. He will not be able to take advantage or a "one-on-one" situation (if he bounces the ball) even though B has cleared-out for him. He is "dead." Players should save the bounce or the dribble until they need it. Make the ball do the work! The ballplayer who bounces the ball as soon as he receives it usually does so because he needs time to think. Bouncing the ball to gain time to think is a bad habit. The dribble should be used to drive, when required by a weave pattern, and when freezing the ball.

11. *Dribbling is an emergency measure! Bring your own ball.* . . .

"Nine out of ten players dribble or bounce the ball before they do anything else!" This is a bad habit and bad basketball because it limits a player's play opportunities. An example:

12. *Talk to your teammates! I've got a secret.* . . .

"Talking on the offense and on the defense builds teamplay!" Talking encourages teammates and a little verbal pat on the back goes a long way. Talking on the defense is vital when picking up loose opponents and calling "stay" and "switch." Words of praise for a good play or effective offensive or defensive rebounding makes for a close knit team. However, a player should not be a traffic cop, should not stand in the back court and tell his teammates what to do. . . .

13. *Never turn your head on defense! The girl in the balcony.* . . .

"A player should never turn his head to watch the ball when playing man-to-man defense." And, conversely, he shouldn't turn his back on the ball when playing on the offense. Naturally, there are times when screens and picks force a defensive player into a situation where the rule must be violated. Then, a teammate must help out. When a player changes from offense to defense, he should back-pedal so that he can locate his personal opponent; point out a loose man; or help out in stopping the opponents' fast break. And, when changing from defense to offense, players should keep their eyes on the ball. Every fan and coach can recall a game incident in which a player who was changing from defense to offense turned his back on the ball only to miss a pass and lose the ball for his team.

14. *Don't cross your feet on the defense! Why move so many feet. . . .*

"Players should move only one foot at a time in defensive play!" Many players move their feet in short steps when playing defense. Moving both feet almost at the same time is bad because it gives the offensive opponent a chance to beat the defensive player. The defensive player should move only one foot at a time so he will be in position to come back to a good defensive position or "go" with his opponent. A defensive player should not cross his feet on defense; especially on the first step. He should shuffle his feet because he can go just as fast shuffling as running sideways and crossing his feet.

15. *Hands up on the defense! Shake hands with yourself. . . .*

"Keeping the hands up is important to body balance and good defense." All offensive players dislike being harassed. Movement of the hands and feet discourages passing and shooting and, often, discourages the opponent. Besides, it shows that the defensive player is *on the ball! Wants* to play ball! And, *wants* the ball! Further, use of the hands when guarding an opponent who does not have the ball discourages a pass to him and makes it difficult for him to move where he wants to go. There was never a good defensive player who didn't use his hands. A tight-rope walker uses his hands to balance his body and the good defensive player does likewise. Hands up!

16. *Watch your opponent's belly button! The handle of the bread basket. . . .*

"Where the belly button goes . . . he goes!" We like our defensive players to keep their eyes glued to a part of the offensive ball player that can't fool them . . . the belly button! It is possible to watch an opponent's number, but there is always the danger of looking up; watching the eyes. We could say: "Watch the belt buckle!" But we prefer to use the belly button because we think it is expressive and easy to

remember. An opponent can fake a defensive player with his
eyes, head, shoulders and feet, but wherever the belly button
goes . . . the opponent must go. When playing against a corner man, the defensive player should be turned a little so he
can watch the ball, but above all . . . he should keep low and
concentrate chiefly on his opponent.

17. *Pick up the first man! First come—first served.* . . .

"Pick up the first man down the floor whether he is your man
or not!" When you are back or coming down the floor ahead of
the rest of your teammates, pick up the first opponent and call
out to the teammate who is closest to *your* man and thus
trade opponents. Some players point to the first man down the
floor and yell for the assigned teammate to take him. However,
the assigned teammate may be caught in a tangle; may have
tried to follow-in; or find it impossible to catch up. So, the first
player down the floor must take the opponent, to save points
and show he is part of the team. Any defensive player looks
silly letting an opponent go down the floor unguarded just
because he is not the man's *assigned* guard.

18. *Don't leave your feet on defense! Dead Indian no
    good.* . . .

"Once a defensive player leaves his feet he is helpless!" We
have an expression at Dartmouth: "Dead Indian no good!"
When a player leaves his feet, he is dead, and his opponent has
a real advantage. Why be a jumping-jack just because the opponent with the ball fakes and "pulls the monkey string"? The
defensive player should keep his feet on the floor unless he
is rebounding, jump shooting, jumping for a held ball, or trying to block a shot after the opponent has released the ball.
The good defensive player keeps his head up and his feet on
the floor. When a defensive player is in the air he gets his
teammates up in the air. If he goes for a fake, his opponent will
drive. . . . Why be a "dead Indian"?

19. *Get position for rebounds! Position is everything in life. . . .*

"Most players could get position for rebounds if they tried!" Many players stand around like dopes when the ball is going up toward the basket. Instinct, and sensing the direction of the shot and the angle of the rebound off the backboard, will enable a player to move into the correct rebounding position at once. Many times the opponent's eyes will tip the defensive player off to the angle at which the ball is coming off the board. Offensive players should hustle for position instead of watching the ball until it is too late. If the offensive player gets position, he should try to tap the ball into the basket or back up on the backboard. Sometimes a fake can be used to get position. If a tap-in or possession is impossible, the long back tap should be attempted.

20. *If you can't rebound you can't win! Join the union. . . .*

"You could almost, though not quite, say that basketball today is: Rebound and shoot!" A team must rebound, however, or it will not get the chance to shoot. Players do not necessarily have to be tall, but it is vital that they block their opponents out, and . . . *want* to rebound. Too many players let the other fellow do it! If a player finds he is the loose man; if he is not being blocked out; or if his man stays out instead of following-in, he should always rebound. We have a mythical organization on our team. We call it the "Union." The big men must make double figures (number of rebounds) to warrant membership. The little men must average six rebounds per game to qualify. "Why did we lose? That's simple! The other guys out-rebounded us!" Block out and REBOUND! Good rebounding affects the other team's shooting. They know they will not get another shot and the pressure is on the shooter. Good rebounding helps a team's own shooting and enables it to get two or three shots to the opponents' one. Good rebounding also limits the opponents' shots. This is the "key" to winning games.

21. *The first fast-break pass must be perfect! A good beginning . . . a perfect ending. . . .*

"You either have the fast break or you don't!" The fast break must get started with the outlet pass—at once! If the first fast-break pass is a good one, the fast break is under way. Once the fast break is started, it is hard to stop. That's why the first pass is so important. A *bad* first pass will bring on another and another and a team usually ends up losing the ball (certainly losing the fast break opportunity). Get off right with a good outlet pass! Wheel it!

22. *You must make 70 per cent of your free throws! Look a gift horse in the mouth. . . .*

"Free throws are more important today than at any other time in the history of basketball!" The value of free throws has been increased chiefly because of the bonus free-throw. It is possible to be outscored from the field but still win the game through greater accuracy from the line. There is no excuse for being a poor free-throw shooter. Practice, confidence, and the proper technique is the key. On the basis of team play, good free-throw shooting upsets the other team and gives your teammates confidence. Players should use the free-throw method natural to them and the one which gets best results. (I give a trophy each year to the best free-throw shooter on my team.) Get that *"one-and-one!"*

23. *Keep the defense busy! It's hard to "move" on the bench. . . .*

"Keep moving to keep the defense busy!" If all five men keep moving, their opponents cannot afford to sag or float. Moving with or without the ball forces the defense into making mistakes since the offensive players know what they are trying to do and the defensive players do not know what to expect. The offensive team which moves, keeps the opponents worried about their defense, and this stress upon defense affects their offense.

24. *Don't cross the backboard to shoot! You take the high
    road.* . . .

"Many players cross the backboard to take a shot with their
favorite hand." This is a definite weakness because the big
objective is to get to the basket quickly and to get the shot
away. A defensive player can catch up with the "cross-over"
shooter because of the extra distance and the time required to
cross over. Further, once an opponent finds out a player likes
a certain hand for shooting, he will over-play his opponent and
make it difficult for him to get *any* shot. A player should learn
to shoot from both sides of the basket, and, with both hands.
Shoot with the left hand from the left side of the basket and
with the right from the right side of the basket.

25. *Never underrate an opponent! Tall trees fall hard.* . . .

"Every game is *THE* Game!" This is more true today than
at any other time. Years ago a five point lead, with ten minutes
to go, was *BIG*. Today, a twenty point lead with ten minutes to
go does not mean the game is on ice! All teams start off playing
better against an opponent if they think they are considered
pushovers. But, if they turn out to be better than anticipated,
even the great team can be upset. So, it is wise to *never* underrate or underestimate an opponent. If they are not as good as
expected, you have lost nothing. Overconfidence can affect a
team's play and it is wise to remember that it is *only the under-
dog* who can do the upsetting. Be ready!

26. *Practice does not always make perfect! Do it right.* . . .

"Practice does not make perfect if you practice the wrong
techniques!" Players often work long and hard and make little
or no progress because they are practicing incorrectly. Stop
them! Start all over! They will make better progress. In this
connection, it is wise to supervise all practices (including three-
man games). Start them right and keep them right! In shooting,
start all practices with lay-ups. Too many players start with long
shots which they will never use in a game. Further, players

acquire poor offensive and defensive habits when fooling
around; they get in the habit of carelessness. Correct practice
of a skill or a play can be just as enjoyable as doing something
half-heartedly or practicing silly stunts. Cut out the French
pastry and stick to bread and butter!

1

The Coach's Homework

A coach has to decide what is to be done and tell somebody to do it! Then he has to listen to reasons why it should not be done or why it should be done in a different way. Or when it is not done, he has to listen to the excuse why it was not done. He again points out how it should have been done and then concludes that maybe he had better forget the whole thing. . . .

PROFESSIONAL RESPONSIBILITIES

Administration: The administrators of the school and of the athletic program determine the philosophies and policies which the coach must observe *without equivocation.* When a fellow accepts a job it is *his* responsibility to accept the conditions and observe the rules and regulations under which he works without the slightest deviation.

Faculty: Each boy at Dartmouth has a faculty advisor and I try to keep contact with him. I try also to keep on friendly terms with all the members of the faculty although it must be kept in mind that not all members of the faculty may be friendly to athletics.

Students: Students may watch our practice any time they wish, and I continually ask them to keep me advised of good basketball players from their home towns. By keeping this relationship with the students they feel that they are part of our team, and are anxious to recommend good ball players.

Their recommendations are usually good because they are fully aware of our scholastic requirements.

Public: I make myself available to the public whenever possible. Public relations are very important. It is important that the coach make himself available to civic organizations and clubs for speaking engagements. I spend many hours with local fans who may wish to sit down for coffee and talk about our program. It is important to get to know and talk with as many local people as possible and it is unwise to neglect local fans for out-of-towners who may seem to be more important.

Publicity: Newspaper publicity is important to our over-all program. I make it a point to be available to newspaper, radio and TV men who may wish to contact me regarding my team or any phase of the game. I always try to get to the pre-game meetings which are held in Boston, New York, and other cities where Dartmouth is to play. It is a good idea to save a good "talking point" for these meetings. A good way to keep the members of the press in your corner is to give them an item which they can feature. I always make it a point to talk to writers following a game.

COACHING RESPONSIBILITIES

Analyzing the schedule: The Ivy League schedule is drawn up two years at a time by the athletic administration. Non-league games cannot be added until the league is taken care of. I center my special plans around the league games in preparing for the season, but I do not overlook the important non-league games.

Team Travel Plans: The travel plans are made up by the senior and junior managers in consultation with the director of athletics.

Scouting Plans: No one man does all our scouting. We think scouting is so important that we secure the best men possible to do the job. Our scouting itinerary is made up as soon as we can get the schedules of our opponents. I do not like to have a team scouted earlier than one week before our game. I feel that it is important that the scout know enough about our own team to decide which of our offensive and defensive maneuvers will work best against a particular opponent.

Scouting is recognized by coaches as an important phase of the coaching profession and there is no secrecy or breach of ethics in the practice. The actual scouting is not so important as the application of the material to the team in preparing for the game. I usually work over the scouting outline and develop tactics which I believe will be most effective in meeting the opponent. When these notes have been arranged, I turn them over to my assistant who familiarizes the reserves with the opponent's offense and defense. Then, we devote one or two practices against the reserves who simulate (as nearly as possible) the tactics of the opponent.

Inspection of Equipment: All equipment is inspected in the spring of each year. Old equipment is discarded and new equipment purchased. Before the new season opens the new equipment is tried out by the players involved. Each boy is allowed to order the type of playing shoe he wishes so he will have no psychological complaint.

Offense Check List: This must be made up prior to the season and included in the regular pre-season practices. The basic offense (in our case the pivot offense); the Three Out-Two-In; the press; the zone press; and last but not least, the zone offense (we stick with one particular type).

Defense Check List: This is also made out before the season starts and included in the practice outline. Straight man to man; switching man to man; two types of zone defense; combination man to man and zone; applying the man-to-man and the zone press; and stopping the fast break. Special defenses are taken up when the need occurs.

Players: I want my players to have the desire to learn and the desire to win; players who will train and sacrifice interfering pleasures for the opportunity to make the team. Next in importance is fighting spirit, hustle and speed.

I try to keep the proper relationship between myself and

the players at all times. I do not think you should be aloof or too distant, yet it is wise not to get too close. There is a happy medium that can be established.

Not all players can be treated exactly the same. Some must be prodded, some must be left almost alone. Remember—each player possesses a different personality and this must be taken into consideration in dealing with him. The team captain must be the liaison man between coaches and players. Captains sometimes turn out to be not as good as some newcomers the next season.

If you have the proper relationship with your captain, you will appreciate this little conversation I had with one of my captains several years ago.

"Coach," he said, "I've often heard you say a captain can be as important to the team on the bench as on the floor. Right?"

I said: "That's right."

He said: "Well, I believe that, too, and I want you to know that I'll be fighting just as hard on the bench as on the floor, if you think that's where I belong."

Boys appreciate the interest of the coach in their physical well-being and other problems. This feeling should be fostered. It is not enough that they respect you for your basketball knowledge and experience; they should feel confident of your desire to help them with other problems.

Returning players, veterans and sophomores should be analyzed at least a year head. You should give careful consideration to the progress the upperclassmen make in the final tough weeks of the current year's campaign so you can decide what use they may be in the rebuilding program for the next season. The coach should continually evaluate the freshman group on the basis of their possibilities as sophomores and carefully consider all sophomores who will be coming up in key spots as starters.

I like to meet the players off the court on a free and easy basis so they will not be afraid to come to me with their problems. Keeping a light heart and letting the boys realize you appreciate a little fun is important. I remember one time I gave my team a hard going-over before a tough game; how a team had to be tough; "do or die" killers; etc. And how "nice" boys lost too easily. Well, we lost the game. Afterwards, one of the players met me and said:

"We sure are nice boys, eh, Coach?"

A coach can have fun and still keep the respect of his players. Along that line, my son Toby, who played for me at Dartmouth and who was graduated several years ago, still calls me "Coach."

I never make a federal case out of a boy's mistake. I tell him what was wrong, make sure he understands and then forget it. If I can have fun in my coaching and develop confidence, poise, and skill in my players, I feel I have been greatly rewarded. A couple of little stories may accentuate this point.

One year Holy Cross was playing against Oklahoma and the Westerners had a great player by the name of Tucker. Tucker had spent two years in the army. He lined up against George Kaftan, our young star and main hope, and said: "Hiya, kid! I hear you got thirty the other night. Let's see what you get tonight!"

Kaftan grinned and said: "Sure, Tucker, but I think you ought to realize that basketball is a young man's game."

Sometimes you can't develop a boy's poise. Most of us have seen practices where the reserves "kill" the varsity. Our reserves always wear blue shirts at practices and one time, just before an important game, they really clobbered the starters. So, in order to sober up the varsity, I started the reserves in the big game. Well, they couldn't do anything right. So I called for a time out and I said: "You guys forgot your blue shirts!"

Cutting the squad is the toughest thing to do. One year I just couldn't make up my mind. I made a list and put down zeros and X's to select the squad. Someway, I got them all mixed up. . . . So I said: "The heck with it! I'll bring them all back for another coupla practices." Ever happen to you?

Scholastic Studies: They represent, after all, the chief purpose for school attendance. The attitude of the coach toward the value of study and the necessity for application can influence and help the player. All too frequently boys become so wrapped up in sports that nothing else seems to matter. Every effort should be made to help these boys change their attitudes.

"If you can't pass, you can't play," applies first to school and second to basketball.

Practice: "Stop at the peak!" A mountain climber wants to get to the top of the mountain. When your boys are doing exceptionally well in practice, *stop!* "How much rice can a Chinaman eat?" Do not continue with the particular work or drill or practice if it spells drudgery! If you keep going, your players will only get worse. This is true of scrimmage or anything else you may be doing. For example, today we'll say the team is scrimmaging particularly well, making good plays, shooting well, rebounding expertly and playing good defense. Just because you have allotted a certain time to scrimmage, do not keep going. . . . Stop! You want them to carry some of that "go" over to the next day.

When the boys look good we often stand there with a smug feeling of satisfaction, self admiration, thinking: "Boy, I've really got them trained!" The longer you work in this situation, the less they will improve; you will get mad and start hollering at them and pretty soon everybody will be doing things they shouldn't and you'll have scrambled eggs! Stop at the peak! The objective of practice is to develop the mental alertness which enables a player to recognize a given basketball situation and to equip him physically with the proper skills and reactions to apply them promptly and efficiently.

Practice Outlines: I prepare my outlines in detail far ahead of the first practice, making sure I will cover every phase of the game. However, I leave time for certain phases which may need additional work (we work at every practice on shooting, the fast break, and one-on-one).

Drills: I know of no easy way to acquire basketball skills. It takes constant work and practice. In my own opinion, the best way to develop a skill is through the use of drills. Drill work requires perseverance, determination, and never-ending willingness to work and improve.

Conditioning: Pre-season practice by the squad should be anything but basketball, with the exception of shooting and fun games. Calisthenics, practicing the boxer's glide, rope skipping, shadow boxing, squeezing handballs, and working out with a medicine ball will aid in preparing for the season. Cross-country running is a great pre-season conditioner.

During early-season conditioning, the coach should bring his squad along carefully. The use of a number of small medicine balls is just the thing to loosen up the fingers, strengthen the wrists, and provide material for general exercise drill. Bending, turning, and all sorts of passes are possible and the player gets a good workout before the actual practice period begins. (If the school is unable to afford a sufficient number of medicine balls, an excellent substitute may be the use of old discarded basketballs, filled with a heavy substance.)

The health of the players is the first consideration in coaching. Primary decisions with respect to the advisability of athletic participation rests in the hands of a qualified physician. Dartmouth maintains a medical staff which issues certificates that qualify or bar the respective player from athletics. After certification the player is in the hands of the coach.

Training, conditioning, and the individual consideration of each player are the obligations of the coach. Some boys are qualified for heavy work while others are not too strong and must be nursed along carefully. Here, the services of an intelligent trainer are invaluable, not only for training treatments and taping, but for purposes of evaluation of each player's capabilities. "Some players can break training and play a good game but he or you will never know how much better he could have played!"

Training Plans: Conditioning and training plans are prepared in cooperation with the head trainer before the season begins. These include precautions against injuries; taping; medical care for minor ailments; etc. Checking of training facilities is completed before the season with the director of athletics and the person in charge of the playing and training facilities. Changes in facilities, as they occur, are checked with these supervisors.

PHILOSOPHIES

Think: I often walk into a dressing room when we are playing on the road and see a card on the wall with the word

T H I N K printed on it. While I agree that a boy must do some thinking, I also believe he can think too much. A player must make his plays and moves without thinking (subconsciously, so to speak). If he must stop to think, he will be two years too late in doing what he is supposed to do. Frequently, when we are playing badly, I say to the players in the huddle: "Stop thinking so much!"

Desire to Win: My first principle in teaching a boy to play basketball is to instill in him the desire to win. Then it is up to me to teach him *how* to win. I want my players to "want to win," but also to want to gain the respect of their opponents, the officials, the other coaches, the fans and all those persons who believe in sportsmanship. The player must desire to win and must be willing to pay the price for the victory. I shall never teach a boy to win by any questionable method. I want to win fairly or not at all. . . . I think we coaches can help take the softness out of youth growth and substitute a strong physical, mental, and moral fiber. Let's teach these boys team play, responsibility, sportsmanship, quick thinking, the overcoming of fear, and the various physical skills which will benefit them all through their lives.

The Golden Rule: The Golden Rule should be paramount in the mind of everyone who has anything to do with sports. To win graciously and to give full, generous credit to those who defeat us is to be sure we can always feel proud of our efforts and the results. I think we can develop team play when we get across to the boys the importance of a spirit of cooperation or willingness to submerge themselves in and for the group. I like to see a boy who is not only capable of competing with others but able to compete with himself. He will never reach the end but, with God's help, will be forever able to improve. Someone once said, very wisely: "What good is muscle if you lack will? If you lack hustle, what good is skill?" I go for that!

Nothing Succeeds like Success: There is nothing like success to breed confidence. Confidence is a part of growth, and the maturing and direction of growth is the vital element in the coaching profession. An important step in growth is the development of poise. I try to help a boy gain poise by forcing him to substitute deliberate, confident action for nervous impulsiveness. This takes work and thought by the coach as well as the player.

Consistency: A coach always strives for consistency in the play of a boy or of his whole team. Naturally, consistency is something which is almost impossible to teach since it depends so much upon emotional control and concentration. However, by ever keeping after your players to make the correct move, to do it right even when they are fed up, a degree of consistency can be instilled. A story may be apropos at this point. . . .

In my first year as coach of the Boston Celtics I had a center by the name of George Nostrand. Now, George would have his bad nights and when he did he made it a *good* bad one! He was either very good in his play or very bad. This night we were playing the New York Knickerbockers in Providence. It was raining, sleeting, and there was a heavy wind. There weren't four hundred people in the place (most of these were "comps") and nobody, but nobody, cared who won or lost. All through the game you could have heard a pin drop except for one leather-lunged guy who was keeping the crowd entertained more than were the two teams. He was constantly making critical remarks and drawing a lot of laughs.

As I said above, when Nostrand had a bad night—he really had one! They used a gun to end the periods and at the end of the half off goes the gun and in the quiet which followed, out came the voice of this leather-lunged guy: "My God! They *shot Nostrand!*"

Compensation: And when you say: "Let's go!" and the players damn near kill one another reaching in the huddle trying to join hands . . . that's it, brother! That's your compensation and that's why you're a coach!

2

Setting the Table

If the table isn't set, everyone has to wait—the cook, the waitress, the bus boys, the guests, and the family. So, let's start with the offense fundamentals and get ready to enjoy the games.

All coaches realize that a player is no better than his ability to employ the correct fundamentals in a given situation. And we all work on fundamentals from the first day of practice until the last day of the season. Fundamentals are fairly uniform in their application and I do not intend to dwell at great length upon the various techniques. However, I do want to take time to give you my ideas concerning them and their application.

Since all plays are not taught at once, all fundamentals need not be stressed in the beginning. If the coach has planned his practice sessions toward the use of a certain kind of defense, the fundamentals can be developed progressively, one after the other.

Early in the season it is an excellent idea to have some of the veterans or graduate players demonstrate the principles and fundamentals which must be learned. The use of films, when possible, is an ideal method. At Dartmouth, we select one or two films in which the execution of fundamentals and basic plays is outstanding and use them to illustrate the proper techniques. When scrimmages are held during the early practices, they are limited to short sessions and are used chiefly to stress the fundamentals.

At Dartmouth, opportunities for scrimmage against outside

teams are limited. This brings up an important point. Do players progress more rapidly through scrimmage or drill sessions? "Learn by doing" is an old axiom which applies to drill work (on a game basis) as well as to scrimmage. In my opinion, scrimmage can be harmful unless the correct execution of skills has been drilled into the players until they have become habits. At Dartmouth, we never devote more than half of the practice time to scrimmage. No player should scrimmage more than half an hour during practice sessions. And possibly the best results will be obtained when outside teams are used for competition.

Body Balance: This is one of the most important fundamentals in basketball. When a player has body balance he is in a well-poised position and ready to move in any direction. The stance and balance used by professional boxers and wrestlers is probably as good as any other, and players imitate and acquire this style quickly. The arms and legs are flexed in a relaxed position, which means speed in movement and action ("keep 'em loose").

The knees and ankles should be flexed if the player is to maintain correct body balance. Players who are not relaxed and stand stiff-legged will find it impossible to move their bodies quickly enough to make the correct moves. The center of gravity must be lowered to obtain the proper balance and to execute the stops, turns and pivots necessary for good offense and defense.

In one of our important games it appeared to me that Chuck Kaufman should have taken a shot. I asked him, why not? "I was off-balance, Coach," he said. "I was walking a tight-rope!"

Footwork: The ability to move, to shift weight and balance and to out-maneuver a defensive player, or to defend against an opponent, requires proper foot action. Offensively, players must develop correct habits in running, feinting, change of direction, change of pace, and correct use of the pivot.

The good basketball player can stop, turn, pivot, change direction and drive in any direction. But he first must shift his weight in the direction he wishes to go. To break in any direction at top speed the player must keep his body's center of gravity low and learn to quickly shift his weight in the direction he wishes to take.

The Stop: The ability of a cutter or dribbler to stop, in order to secure a good position for a shot or to protect the ball, is important. The player should light on the balls of the feet with the knees spread and flexed and in a slightly forward position, which will permit him to absorb the shock and quickly gain body balance.

Turns and Pivots: These skills follow stops and are easily made if the body balance has been recovered after a stop. To make a turn, the player lowers the shoulder on the side in which he wishes to move. At the same time he pushes off with the opposite foot. Only a little practice is necessary to develop this skill. The efficiency of the pivot depends (as in the turn) upon proper body balance following the stop. In the pivot to the left, the left shoulder will again be lowered and thrust down and back so that the right foot will turn clockwise and to the rear of the left foot. After the start of the pivot the point on the floor at which the right foot lands will determine the degree of the pivot (quarter, half, three-quarter, or full).

 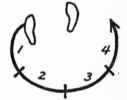

DIAGRAM 3. *Left and Right Pivots.*   (1) Quarter (2) Half (3) Three-quarter (4) Full

Jumping: Leaping can be taught and developed. Most players jump better by standing sideways and executing a slight turn as they leap. The player should concentrate on the ball and allow the official to toss it a little way into the air before leaping. It is wise to remember how high the official tosses the ball (this varies). Timing is important here and leaping too soon or too late means a bad jump.

Faking: Faking with the eyes, head, shoulders and feet (with or without the ball) is an important personal skill. Most players fake naturally while others need much practice to develop the skill. I have found "one-on-one" and "two-on-two" practices an ideal method to develop faking (also playing "dummy"). When I want my kids to fake I often use the expression: "Do it for Sweeny!" They know what I mean.

When I was coaching the Boston Celtics, I used "Do it for Sweeny!" quite a bit during the pre-season practices. Finally, one of the rookies trying out for the team turned to one of the veterans and asked: "Who is this guy, this Sweeny? I haven't seen him yet!" The story? Yes, it's absolutely true!

Passing: Good passing is the bread and butter of strong offensive teams! And, when they are patient, they usually get the shot they want. Good screening, cutting and dribbling coupled with movement of the ball spells trouble for any defense.

Passes should be short and snappy. Slow, lob passes are easy to intercept. Many players, however, get so engrossed in fast passes that they try to force their passes. Then, they are really in trouble. One way to make sure passes will reach the team-mate safely is to teach your players to "beat the pass!" This means that the cutter should put on full speed so that he can get away from his opponent and meet the pass in a good position for a shot.

Joe Mullaney, present Providence College Coach, and a good one too, pulled off a fine stunt. We were practicing at Holy Cross and the boys were a little lazy. I'm yelling, "Move to beat the pass," all afternoon. (I use the word beat instead of meet because of the reverse cut.) Joe was an excellent passer, with either hand, and a real good feeder. This particular practice he was hitting Bob Cousy, now with the Boston Celtics (the greatest little man in the game), quite a bit, and the "Couz," as we used to call him, kept picking them off and throwing in some shots that were really out of this world. Finally, "Couz" cut and Joe threw one clean out of bounds and over everything else in sight. As he threw it he yelled: "Let me see you beat that one, Couz!"

Use of the fingertips with a strong wrist snap and a strong follow-through is the stamp of a good passer. The passer is responsible for making good passes and he is also responsible for interceptions by opponents.

Fancy passes are taboo! Your players must be sure *not* to pass across in front of the opponents' basket at any time. This is the most dangerous pass in the game and the interceptions come (naturally) when a basket is precious.

Flat-footed receivers should be ignored. Basketball is a moving game (players as well as the ball).

Many slow-thinking players bounce the ball as soon as they get it. This is folly. It limits the player's offensive effectiveness and it allows his opponent to play him aggressively and tie up the ball. A habit even more dangerous is passing to a team-mate's back and using blind passes (looking in one direction and passing the opposite way at the same time).

Fumbling: A common fault with many players is the fumble. While many fumbles are caused by poor passing (too high, too low and too hard), the chief fault lies with the receivers. Most fumbles are caused by player fatigue, fighting the ball, and loss of temper. The hands should be cupped and the ball should be allowed to "flow" into the fingers accompanied by "give" of the hands, wrists and elbows. The consistent fumbler should be taught to watch the ball right into his hands.

The dribble: Learning to dribble the ball is merely a matter of desire by the player. It is the one skill which can be practiced almost anywhere and without help—at home, on the back porch or on the playground. The player should learn to dribble with his head up and with his eyes focused ahead on his team-mates or the opponents.

When dribbling for speed the bounce is made belt-high and with the body in an upright position. When the dribble is being used to escape from a tight situation or for control, the body is bent over and the bounce should not rise above knee-level.

Use of the eyes, head and shoulders are important in keeping the dribbler's opponent off balance. The change-of-pace and trapping the ball (lowering the dribbling hand and meeting the ball on the up-bound) are important skills of the expert dribbler. The dribble blends in well with the fast break and is an important set offensive weapon (with screening, driving-in on a one-on-one situation, setting up plays, advancing against the press and freezing the ball).

Screening: The use of screens, moving and set, is imperative in developing a set attack. In the moving screen, the screener should attempt to get in as close to his teammate's opponent as possible without making contact (charging). In the set screen, the screener can set his screen in front, behind or at the side of an opponent. When using a moving screen, the screener should move in a loose, bent-over position so he can change direction quickly. When applying a set screen the screener can be more erect, but ready for contact. Here, the screener should stand immobile without swaying or moving his arms and hands. (Remember the three-foot rule.)

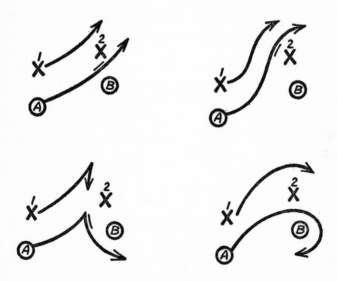

DIAGRAM 4. *Back Court Screens.* Attacking players A and B here execute inside, outside and back screens. (Note the change of direction and maneuvering which is designed to conceal the actual direction of the screen being executed.)

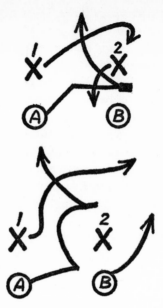

DIAGRAM 5. *Set Screens.* On set screens, always be ready to use the front give-and-go should the opponents make a mistake.

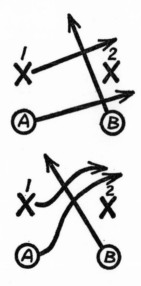

placed so that the teammate can come right off the screener's tail.
DIAGRAM 6. *Moving Screens.* On moving screens, the screen should be

Cutting: Hard cutters play havoc with man-to-man and zone defenses alike. The cutter should use change of pace, change of direction, and develop a hard driving style of cutting. Lowering the shoulder away from the ball will enable the cutter to watch for a pass as he drives toward the basket.

The smart offensive player uses his teammates and the opponents as screens and blocking posts into which he can maneuver his opponent when driving to the basket. Naturally, the clever cutter will drive for the ball or the basket when his opponent turns his head to watch the ball.

When a player starts a cut, he should go through with it. If he does not receive a pass he can cut to the opposite corner (away from the ball).

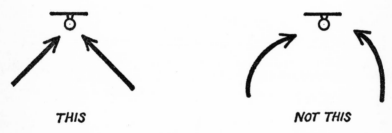

THIS   **NOT THIS**

DIAGRAM 7. *Cutting.* When cutting to the basket, the forty-five degree angle (45°) should be used rather than a curve as shown above.

Play-Making: I always try to prepare a play-maker a year in advance. When this is impossible I look for one at the very first practice. The player I am looking for is one who can recognize play situations, who can grasp the potential of a situation in a fraction of a second. This player may be using the give-and-go, the screen (toward or away from a teammate), yet, in that short fraction, be able to decide whether to go through with the play or cancel it out.

One of the secrets of play-making is to eliminate unnecessary players in the action. There isn't a play in basketball that can't be set up with three men. The good play eliminates the unnecessary men but manages to maneuver them into action which will keep *all* the opponents busy. An example follows:

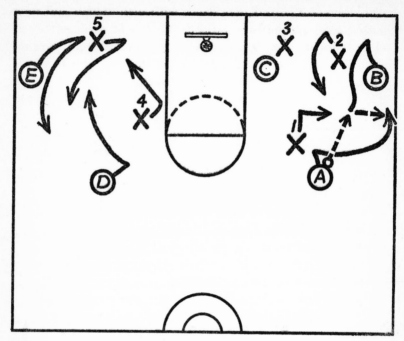

DIAGRAM 8. *Keeping Opponents Busy.* While players A, B, and C are setting up the play above, teammates D and E stay out of the play but change positions with appropriate fakes to keep their defensive opponents busy.

Offensive Rebounding: Getting the ball off the offensive board following an unsuccessful shot is important. Most teams try to follow-in after a shot, and if they find that their defensive opponents turn their heads to watch the ball or fail to block out, the attacking team is in luck. In addition, a strong follow-in attack will help to throttle the opponents' fast break.

Shooting: A good boxer knows when to jab, when to throw a right punch, a hook, an uppercut, etc. The basketball player must also know when to use one of his shots. Too often I see a player take the wrong shot at a critical time. Whether it be the layup, the jump, the set, or the hook, players must be taught the importance of using the right shot at the right time.

I once asked a world's champion pocket billiard player how he decided what shot to make next. He said: "I always shoot the ball closest to the pocket. The shorter the distance the less chance I have to miss."

The following points are stressed at Dartmouth in teaching shooting:

1. Good body balance is important. The player should get his balance quickly, square his shoulders, hips and feet to the basket and, on a "clean" shot, focus his eyes on a point which bisects the edge of the rim nearest to him. He should keep his eyes focused on this point before and following the release of the ball. The purpose is, of course, to determine a straight line. The arc and force which must be applied to the ball to insure a slight clearance of the point on the ring must come through practice.

2. All players should know the floor positions from which they are most accurate in their shooting and practice moving from spot to spot so they will know immediately whether they should use a clean shot or "bank" the ball.

3. The player should "see" the shot before he releases the ball; he should estimate the distance, the arc, and the amount of power necessary to reach the basket. Then, and only then, should he release the ball.

4. The shooter should get the ball away quickly. But he should be sure he has developed the proper techniques until they are second nature.

5. The player must shoot with confidence; he must feel sure he is going to "hit" and all that is necessary is to reach up to the basket and drop the ball through the hoop.

6. The shooter should spin the ball. A spinning ball indicates control, and control means accuracy.

7. Follow-through is important. Lifting the head to watch the ball forces the body back and curtails a complete follow through.

8. Good shooters should be team players and prove it by attempting only good shots. If they do not have good positions and good body balance they do not attempt the shot—they *pass* the ball.

The Lay-Up Shot: The ball should come off the finger tips

with the palm toward the backboard. The shooter should get as high off the floor as possible and he should focus his eyes on the "banking" spot on the board. The hand should not roll and he should try to avoid English.

"Doimie" O'Connell, who played for me at Holy Cross, had a tendency to shoot his lay-ups too hard and harsh. Too many times his shot would hit the backboard and rebound back over the rim. George Kaftan, a great jumper and rebound man, was very good at tapping missed shots by his teammates in the basket. This particular night, Doimie was really throwing them up hard. Kaftan had gotten himself three or four baskets on tap-ins. After the last one he said: "Doimie! (he liked to kid Doimie about his New York accent), keep shooting lay-ups and I'll be high scorer!"

One-hand Set-Shot: The arm should be extended fully with the wrist breaking downward on the follow through. The full arm extension should be held for a brief moment after the ball has left the hand. The eyes are focused on the rim.

Two-hand Set Shot: The ball is held just below the eyes a short distance from the body and is released with a full extension of the arms. Just previous to the release, the shooter leaps slightly from the floor (the distance from the basket determines the height of the leap). Again, the eyes are focused on the rim of the basket.

The Jump Shot: The shooter should leap straight up and land where he took off. The ball should be released at the peak of the leap and the wrists should be firm. The ball should be released from the finger tips and the hand should snap through with a free wrist action.

The Hook Shot: The ball should be released from the finger tips in back of the head or over the top but never in front of the face. This shot is usually synchronized with a long step away from the basket. It should be limited to an area no more than fifteen feet from the basket.

Free Throws: If a player is shooting 70 per cent, leave him alone. Otherwise, change his style. In the one- and two-hand set shot from the line, the same principles governing shots from the field are employed. If the two-hand underhand shot is used the ball should be held with the fingers spread, feet at least hip width, knees bent, and with the back held straight. The follow-through should be made with both hands in an upward motion. I always tell my players to try to lift the ball over the rim with their hands and drop the ball through the hoop. I also remind them that "no one is guarding them on free throws!"

Free-throw shooters should concentrate on the target before, during, and after the shot. Some boys get so intent on bouncing the ball on the floor that they forget to look at the basket until just before they shoot. They should look where they're going to shoot and feel that they are going to put their hands through the hoop.

Matty Begovich was officiating a game several years ago at Dartmouth. Matty was a good official, had a lot of common sense, and possessed a fine sense of humor. The other team kept fouling us to get the ball. Finally, I thought one of the fouls was pretty deliberate and I yelled from the bench: "Matty! a deliberate foul! Two shots!" As he went past the bench, looking straight ahead, Matty yelled back: "Just a casual foul, Doggie! Just a casual foul!"

3

Washing the Dishes

The offensive part of basketball is the appetizer, hors-d'oeuvres, the entrée, the salad and the dessert. But someone has to clear the table and wash the dishes. In basketball, that someone is *everyone*. Yes, everyone has to play defense in the round ball game—if you're going to have a good team. So let's get with it and take a brief look at the defense fundamentals.

Basketball offense today is far ahead of defense. The soaring scores of today's games eloquently prove the statement. I often hear a fan say: "Why don't coaches teach defense?" Well, we do! Perhaps not so much as we should but there are certain good reasons why defensive coaching is not so obvious to the fan. First, today's high scoring is not the result of poor defensive coaching; it is the result of greater player shooting-efficiency and the deadly accuracy of the "jump" shot. Second, the great majority of coaches have stressed the fast break with its resulting "quick" score. Third, the publicity given to the high-scoring players has filled every youngster with the urge to be a "scorer" and shooting has taken precedence over every other basketball skill.

Today, we see certain players who, seemingly, cannot be stopped from getting their shots away and from scoring their twenty or thirty or even fifty points in a given game. Further, screening and other set attack methods have made it virtually impossible for a defensive player to stick with his assigned

opponent when his team is using a matching man-to-man
defense. Naturally, coaches have been forced to use sagging,
floating, double-teaming, the press, zones and combinations in
attempting to stop these great scorers. Admitting that these
methods are not as efficient as a tight man-to-man defense, we
still find that their use permits interceptions, congests scoring
areas near the basket, develops double-team possibilities and,
frequently, through surprise shifts, throws the attack off stride.

At Dartmouth the man-to-man defense is taught individually
and to the team. We consider the man-to-man defense to be our
basic defense and the press, the zone, and the other combinations are considered as variations.

At Dartmouth we start our freshmen playing man-to-man
defense. They are taught to concentrate solely on their assigned opponent and are expected to stick with him. The
defensive position is on a direct (straight) line between the
opponent and the basket unless he is in a position close or
under the basket (here we expect the defensive player to play
at the side or in front of the offensive player).

We tell our freshmen to switch only when they are clearly
blocked away from their opponent. Otherwise, they are expected to keep a good defensive position at all times. The
"switch" is always called by the man closest to the basket. To
help the defensive teammate who may be worried about a
screen or a pick behind him, the player closest to the basket
will warn him of a possible switch by saying "heads up" or, if
a switch will not be necessary, calling "stay!" When a switch
is made, the defensive players must be alert to the necessity for
switching back to cover their own men as quickly as possible.

Stance: The proper starting point in teaching defense is the
stance. I prefer the boxer's stance (one foot forward). I believe
this gives the defensive player greater area coverage on the
perpendicular between his man and the basket. When the feet
are parallel, the reverse pivot by either foot covers a backward
distance of approximately three feet. When the boxer position
is used the pivot on the back foot, swinging the front foot back,
covers approximately twice the distance. When a cutter or
driver goes to the side of a defensive man's back foot, he is

already in position and, unlike the defensive player who plays with his feet parallel, does not require a backward step.

Balance: The knees are slightly bent with the trunk leaning slightly forward. The weight is evenly distributed and the center of gravity is lowered so the player can move in any direction without having to first gain balance. The weight is mostly on the balls of the feet but the heels are lightly touching the floor. I like to have the player keep one hand up and one to the side to aid in keeping balance and in discouraging shots and passes. Keeping arms extended is important as it lessens the area available for the offense. "Quick hands" are an important factor in defense.

Floor Positions: With few exceptions, the defensive player should be in a direct line between his opponent and the basket. His main concentration, naturally, must be on his assigned man. However, he should try to turn his body so he can also watch without turning his head. When guarding a man in the back court and with the ball behind him, the defensive player doesn't dare turn his head to see the ball. When guarding a man who is moving directly under the basket, he plays in front of his man facing the ball.

Beating an Opponent to Position: In teaching this principle, I draw an imaginary arc of approximately fifteen feet (15) around the basket. In this critical scoring area we encourage our players to play the ball more often. We attempt to play on the side of our opponent to cut off the passing lane between him and the ball and we want our players to contest all passes.

In the areas further from the basket we often concede the pass. In this fifteen foot semi-circle, however, we play the ball hard. When an opponent moves into this area we try to force him to continue out of the area to get the pass or to change his direction away from the ball. Even here, we play in a position between him and the ball until he moves from the area. We admit that this is a gamble and at times will backfire, but we have found it gives us a more aggressive defense and feel that the gain is greater than the loss.

Overshifting: A defensive player may overshift right or left half-a-man or a full-man (determined by the distance the opponent's feet are placed apart). This move is designed to overcome the opponent's tendency to drive only in one direction or to force him to move in a particular direction which may be advantageous to the defense.

Sagging and Floating (Sag Back and Float Across): The "sag off" principle is used by all man-to-man defensive teams when they are not employing the press. Described briefly, this means a defensive player will retreat a little further away from his man and toward the basket where he can help out his teammates should one of their opponents break free for the basket. The distance of this retreat depends upon the situation but should not exceed the distance his opponent is playing away from the ball.

The floater must concentrate upon his opponent at all times and refrain from turning his head to watch the ball. If the ball is passed to his opponent or close to him, the sagging or floating player must approach his man at once and play him closely. Sagging and floating permits a defensive player to try for interceptions (especially against a give-and-go offense).

Talking: Talking is an important defensive fundamental no matter what type of defense is used. Talking builds team spirit, cooperation, and defensive understanding. Talking is vital in calling for a switch, in avoiding blocks, pickoffs, and general defensive confusion. For example, a player may not realize that his opponent has completed a dribble and is holding the ball while getting ready to make a pass. A teammate may call out: "He's dead!" so the man with the ball can be rushed thus limiting his time in taking a shot or passing to a teammate.

One afternoon I discussed at great length the importance of talking. A little later during a scrimmage I heard one of the players call: "Switch!" The play was perfectly executed and I was delighted. Then I heard the player who had been trapped say: "Thanks for helping me out!" The player who had called the switch said: "Never mind the thanks. Pay me the two bucks you owe me!"

Hands and Arms: A defensive team whose players keep their hands and arms up to the fullest extent is difficult to outmaneuver. Many fine teams use the slogan "Hands up!" when

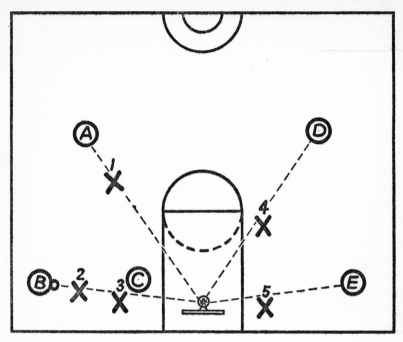

DIAGRAM 9. *Man-to-Man Defensive Positions.* Defensive player X-1 is observing the "in-line" principle (note that he has dropped away from his opponent A so that he will not be outrun to the basket). Defensive player X-2 has overshifted to his left to protect the end line. (Over-shifting is sometimes effective when opposing a player who ordinarily cuts or dribbles consistently to one side or in one direction.) Defensive player X-3 is playing in a semi-front position so that the man with the ball B will have difficulty passing the ball to the pivot player C. Defensive player X-4 has sagged back from offensive player D. Note that X-4 has sagged back to a position where he can watch his opponent as well as the ball without turning his head. Defensive player X-5 has floated away and back toward the end line so he can also watch his opponent E and the ball without turning his head.

on the defense to discourage opponents' shots and passes. Correct use of the hands leads to many interceptions. Pointing out to designate an opponent is an important defensive gesture and enables teammates to quickly size up the defensive situation.

Fully extended arms increase the guarding area and help to clog up the scoring area. If a teammate has been lost in the offensive shuffle and his opponent is breaking for the basket, the waving of both hands above the head frequently results in deflecting a pass.

Guarding the man with the ball: When an opponent has the ball, the defensive player moves one, two, or three arms length away from him, depending upon the situation and his position on the court. If the opponent is a driver as well as a poor "outside" shooter, as much as three arms length away may be permitted. However, I prefer that my players play the player with the ball aggressively.

Guarding the man without the ball: As in guarding the man with the ball, a defensive player may drop off his opponent. However, if this particular man is the opponents' quarterback, he should be played closely to limit his opportunity to get the ball. Here, good use of the hands is important in discouraging passes to the quarterback by his teammates.

It is also important that the defensive player who is guarding an opponent without the ball help out in the general team defense. He can be alert to try for interceptions and double-team opportunities. Further, he can shift to close up the paths to the basket and often make a successful stab at the ball when a dribbler or post or pivot player is near.

Guarding the dribbler: One of the most prevalent weaknesses of the defensive players who are guarding a dribbler is the tendency to play the ball instead of the man. A grab at the ball is exactly what the expert dribbler wants. It is far better to concentrate on the "belt buckle" and force the dribbler away from the basket.

Guarding the pivot man: The big problem in basketball is the big man. Many teams have two and sometimes three big men and certain defensive "privileges" are permitted. Zone defenses, double-teaming, sagging and floating are some of the methods used to stop the dangerous pivot scorer. At Dartmouth we coach our big men to play in front and on the side of the pivot player determined by the movement of the ball. We also try to pinch off the passing lanes between the ball and the big man.

The defensive player should *never* stand directly behind a

big man who is in a set position near the basket. He should move in front of him or take a position at the side of the man nearest the ball. By moving and using the hands to discourage passes the big man may often be forced away from the basket.

Interception and deflecting opportunities are often present when the big man is guarded from the front or side. However, care should be taken in trying for the interception or deflection since a false move may result in an easy basket or a foul.

Slide and Front, Switch and the Defensive Roll: Practically every team today employs screening and "pick" tactics. The use of these offensive techniques has made it imperative that man-to-man defensive measures such as slide, front and switch or some form of the zone be used to meet them. In the man-to-man defense, the slide is used to move quickly between a teammate and his man in trying to keep up with an offensive opponent. Going "front" means that the defensive player follows his opponent and slides in front of a teammate's man. The switch is used when a defensive player is blocked away from his opponent and the help of a teammate is needed to cover him. The switch should be used only when it is impossible to fight through the screens and should always be called by the back man (the defensive player closest to the basket).

At Dartmouth, each player tries to stay with his own man when using the man-to-man defense, and switch only when it is absolutely necessary. However, we encourage aggressive switching to the man with the ball if there is an opportunity of getting a piece of the ball. This is particularly true in the area close to the basket.

Switching must be decisive and quick. Once a switch is called, the players involved must go through with it whether they think the switch is right or wrong. Otherwise, they will wind up with two men on one.

Blocking-out: A good defensive player knows where his opponent is at all times. This is just as important after a shot as before. When a defensive player turns to watch the ball following a shot without blocking-out his opponent, he usually leaves one of his unfortunate teammates with two opponents on his

DIAGRAM 10. *Slide and Front*. On the left side of the court above, offensive player B has cut close in front of his teammate D and defensive player X-2 is forced to use the "slide" to stick with his opponent. On the right, offensive player A has attempted to maneuver defensive player X-1 into the pick set by opponent C. However, A left room for X-1 to "stay" with him and a slide or switch was unnecessary.

back. One potential shot by the opponents is bad enough. Two or three shots are impossible. You can't win!

All defensive players are expected to move between their respective opponents and the basket as soon as a shot is taken and then to move with their man so that they *remain* between him and the rebounding ball. In doing this, the defensive player must make sure that he does not get pushed under the basket where he will have no chance to get the ball.

As soon as the opponents take a shot the defensive player should use the half-pivot in the shortest direction so he can box out his opponent as well as keep his eye on the ball. Then, as the opponent moves, he can move so that he keeps his position be-

DIAGRAM 11. *The Switch and the Defensive Roll.* On the left side of the court shown above, offensive player B has cut hard and close to the pivot man E. Defensive player X-5 sees that teammate X-2 will not be able to keep up with opponent B and calls "Switch!" Now, X-5 switches to guard B and defensive player X-2 covers E. On the right side of the court, offensive player A has maneuvered his opponent X-1 into the pivot man thus forcing a switch. Defensive player X-3 calls "Switch!" and quickly picks up A. Defensive player X-1 now uses the defensive roll to get into position to guard the pivot player.

tween him and the ball. The elbows should be spread and carried high with the feet apart and with the center of gravity carried low. The defensive rebounder must now keep his position against pressure by the opponents and be prepared to leap high for the ball at the right time.

When a defensive player is guarding an outside man he should watch the opponent's eyes as soon as the shot goes up (only exception to watching the belt buckle). Then, the defensive player can drop back toward the basket to help out if his opponent does not follow-in. Watching the opponents' eyes often tips off the direction the ball is taking on the rebound.

DIAGRAM 12. *Rebounding Positions.* The broken circle represents the area in which most rebounds fall and it is important that the defensive players inside this circle do a good job of boxing-out their opponents and getting into position to make the rebound. As shown above, defensive players X-3, X-4, and X-5 are concentrating on boxing-out C, D and E and getting into position for the rebound. Defensive players X-1 and X-2 have dropped back and are moving with their opponents A and B.

When an opponent is going for his basket all by himself and is far ahead of everybody and it looks like it will be an easy two points, I still want my players to chase him. I keep yelling, "The ball may hit a rock!" I want my boys to chase after him so that they will be there to get the rebound in case the shot is missed. (I've seen plenty of them missed both ways!) One day we were practicing a fast break drill, working especially on hitting the lay-out man. George Raming, a 6'-5", 220 pound boy, was getting a good workout since we were trying to get him in shape. He was coming up the floor real fast and looking to get the pass and then I heard a thump. There was George—flat on his face on the floor. "What happened, George?" I asked. "I guess I hit a rock, Coach," he said.

The Rebounders' Union: Several years ago we were playing Vermont at Burlington on a Tuesday and Houston at Hanover on a following Thursday so we came right back after the game at Vermont (100 miles). We had made arrangements for our after-game snack about 20 miles out of Burlington.

I let them have pie a-la-mode for dessert. Well, when the team finished eating they asked me if they could have more ice cream. (Ivy Leaguers can really eat!) I said: "I'll tell you what I'll do. If you beat Houston on Thursday we'll treat you to all the ice cream you can eat."

Rudy La Russo, my big boy now with Los Angeles, jumped right up and said: "There will be a rebounders' union meeting right away!" Right there the rebounders' union was born.

In order to belong to the union, *all* players had to qualify. Big men had to get double figures in rebounds, little men, six rebounds. Well, believe me, fellows, just that thought on La Russo's part did us a lot of good. The kids, believe it or not, tried desperately in every game to qualify for the union. If they made it in any particular game they would come rushing into the dressing room, saying: "Coach, I made the rebounder's union!"

If we bogged down in our rebounding in a game, I'd say to Rudy (in front of the squad): "You had better call a rebounders union meeting, Rudy."

A funny thing happened in one of the games a little later that year. Rudy, by far my top rebounder, came up with only eight rebounds one night. In fact, the entire team had a poor night on rebounds. So, next day, I said: "Rudy, you had better call a rebounders meeting!" The rest of the team gleefully chirped up: "He can't, Coach! He is temporarily suspended!"

Offensive Rebounding: In trying to get an inside position on an opponent, the offensive player can apply pressure one way and go the other. He should fake one direction and then step around his opponent with his inside leg. Another method is to force the opponent under the basket through body pressure (this will work against a rebounder who stands upright while waiting for the rebound).

Guarding the Out-of-Bounds Player: In guarding an opponent out-of-bounds with the ball, the defensive player should face sideways so he can watch his opponent as well as the other players on the court. The opponent out-of-bounds cannot score until the ball has been passed in to a teammate, so he is not particularly dangerous. However, if the defensive player turns his back on the court and plays his out-of-bounds opponent closely (sometimes necessary in applying the press) a block or pick may be set against him permitting the out-of-bounds player to cut unguarded in-court for a shot. A side position, however, may enable the defensive player to see a play coming, and he can help his teammates by calling out the possibility or he may even be able to break it up.

DIAGRAM 13. *Guarding Out-of-Bounds Player.* Defensive player X-1 is standing in a sideways position between the man out-of-bounds with the ball (A) and the basket. In this position, X-1 can see his opponent, the ball and the players on the court who are closest to the ball. Defensive teammates X-3, X-4, and X-5 have dropped away from opponents C, D and E so they will be prepared for a possible pick.

General Defensive Play: Defensive play can never be taken lightly but I often think of an incident which occurred while I was at Holy Cross. I had been working hard on defense in preparation for our next opponent's high scorer. Just before the game I said: "He doesn't look too tough! My grandmother could handle him!"

However, the "star" was really good and in the game, George Kaftan couldn't hold him. After the star had scored several times, George came by the bench and said: "Better send for your grandmother, Coach!"

4

Man-to-Man Attack
Formations

In all of the plays and offenses we use at Dartmouth, we make it clear to the players that there are no handcuffs on them. We let our players do what they can do best at the right time. If several players are working on a play and one of them sees an opening for a different play which has a good chance of succeeding, he is *encouraged* to give it a try. General Principles:

1. The style of play is varied to comprehend the abilities of the players available.
2. The fast break is vital. All our offensive systems and moves are predicated on the principle that we will fast break every time we get the ball.
3. We will utilize the "protected" slow advance if the fast break is impossible.
4. Speed is the key (movement of the ball and players in the fast break and in the team's offensive play).
5. Basically, the players maneuver and advance into the "wide" formation as soon as they see that the fast break is impossible. Then, one of the offensive formations is set up and the players attempt to work one of that system's plays. However, should a player spot an opening for a personal play or a chance to set up a one-on-one or a two-on-two situation, he is expected to take advantage of the opportunity.

47

6. The players must be sold on the premise that only good shots (preferably "facing" shots) will be attempted, and that forced shots are permissible only in a desperate situation and when there are less than seven seconds left to play in a given situation.

7. The front line players (pivot and corner men) should be tall (height is an advantage in receiving, passing, shooting, following-in, feeding the pivot, general defensive play and defensive rebounding). All front line players should be able to play the pivot position.

8. The back court players should include at least one rebound guard who can play one of the corner positions should the pivot attack be used. If he can use give-and-go techniques all the better. He should understand the weave and be able to blend into the handling of the ball. A clever floor guard who can serve as the play-maker and quarterback is vital to any offense. This player must be a good passer, feeder, and possess a good outside shot.

The quarterback sets up the offense, usually determines the play by his moves and handling of the ball, and is in charge of the offensive and defensive balance. The third back court player should be an all-around player—a hard cutter, a good passer and be able to score. All of the back court players must be able to move into the various offensive formations without delay and blend into the plays.

ATTACKING THE MAN-TO-MAN DEFENSE

We use the Four-Man Weave and the Five-Man Give-and-Go for circulation purposes and to give us back court protection. These two circulations also give our players a chance to use their personal offense abilities.

The set attacks we use are important in developing our team plays, defensive balance and aid in teaching our players to help one another to break free from the defensive opponents. When the fast break fails, the defense is given a chance to form. Then we size it up and start one of our offenses.

The teaching of a set attack requires patience and hours of

repetitive drill. It is difficult to discipline players so that they will "wait" for the play to develop. Passing and cutting to various positions before attempting a shot seems unnecessary to most players. However, there is no other way to teach team play. Vital to the set offense is a back court quarterback who can set up the offense, get it started on its way, and supervise his teammates' moves until the play is completed.

At Dartmouth, we specialize in two chief set attacks when opposing the man-to-man defense: the "Four-Man Weave with a Pivot" and the "Three-Two." Against zone defenses we prefer the "One-Three-One" set attack.

The Fast Break

The Dartmouth fast break is simple. No crossing—get down the floor and never, never pass the ball back. If forward passing is not possible, we hold the ball and go into our wide formation so that a hurried pass or shot is eliminated. A fumble or interception following a backward pass often results in an easy basket for the opponents since our fast-break players are caught in poor defensive positions. Our drill without defensive opposition follows:

Free-Throw Fast Break

We use the standard "three-lane" fast break and eliminate anything fancy or tricky.

Player B secures the rebound and passes to D on the right sideline. D passes to E in the center of the court. E dribbles hard for the free-throw line. C and D cut as shown and A becomes the trailer. B is safety.

The wing men, C and D, must stay wide. The first lay-out man down the floor goes deep to his corner and then "turns the corner" at a 90 degree angle. The other wing man cuts on a 45 degree angle when he reaches the free-throw line. The trailer (A) usually cuts to the open space left by the defensive player or players who attempt to check the dribbler or the wing men.

The middle man (dribbler) always holds at the free-throw line whether he has the ball or not. The rebounder (B) comes

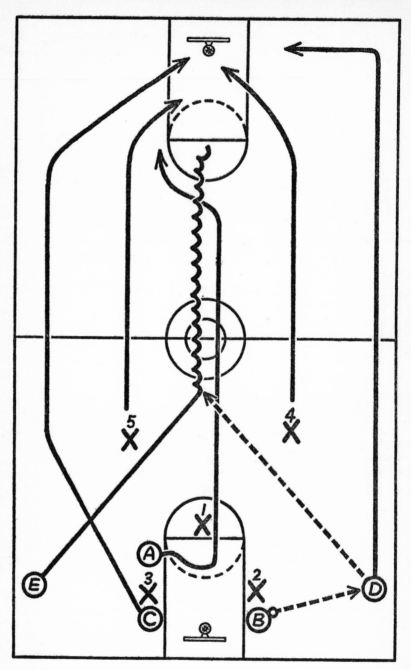

DIAGRAM 14. *Free-Throw Fast Breaks.*

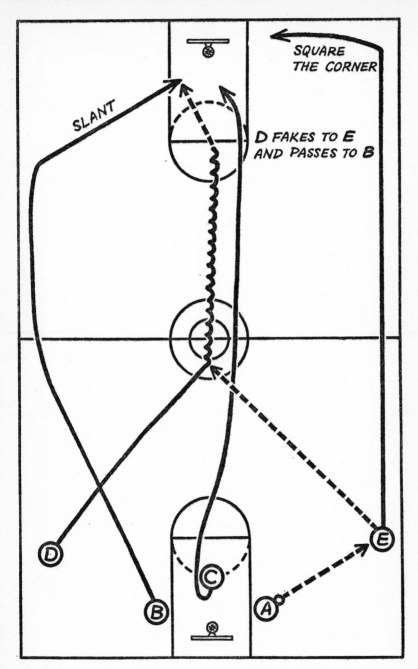

DIAGRAM 15. *Rebound Fast Break.* Here, player D dribbles all the way. Naturally, he can exchange passes with B and E if it is necessary. However, no one *ever* passes back. Ordinarily, the *first* man down drives clear to the corner before moving along the baseline toward the basket. His teammate on the other side of the court slants in toward the lane.

up to the middle of the floor and stops to check the defensive balance and act as a safety valve.

The lay-out men or the wing men, as you wish, may keep the ball. Once we get down to a position near the basket we employ standard fast-break passes.

The first pass must be perfect. We like our rebounder to pass to the lay-out man while he is still in the air following his recovery of the ball from the backboard. Since the best way to stop a fast break is to intercept the ball we make every effort to safeguard the first pass.

Once the first pass is under way we like to "wheel it." If the receiver of the first pass is out in front of this teammates, he does not wait but gets under way with the dribble. The big objective is to get there first with the mostest.

The Slow Advance

If a fast break opportunity is not present, our two back court men will bring the ball up the court by means of short passes, the dribble, or a combination of the two. The corner men keep the same distance between them in their advance so that they may break back to help out should the opponents try some form of the press. Frequently, we employ three men to bring the ball up court in the slow advance so that they may employ a pass-and-go-behind advance if the opponents try the press.

The Wide Formation

Following a fast break which does not succeed in freeing a player for a good shot at the basket, or when a fast break is impossible, our players set up in our wide formation.

We were playing an important game at home one year and my center, George Raming, was having a tough night in the pivot. Late in the game, George decided to take his man "outside." He got into the weave circulation but caused some confusion among his teammates. I was about to wave him back "inside" when I heard the commanding and piercing voice of George's girl. "George!" she yelled. "You get up close to the basket where you belong!"

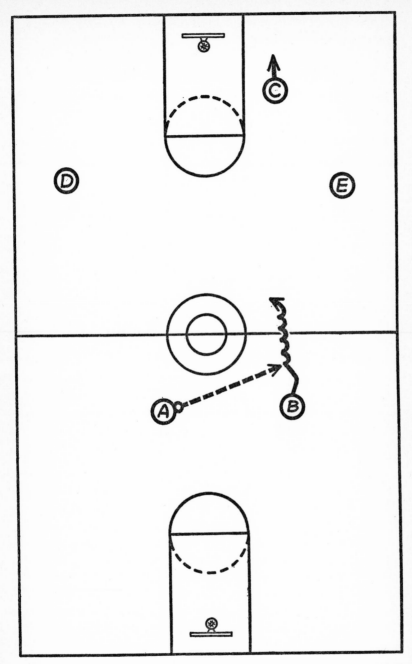

DIAGRAM 16. *The Slow Advance.* C, D and E are watching A and B and are prepared to break back to help them if necessity arises.

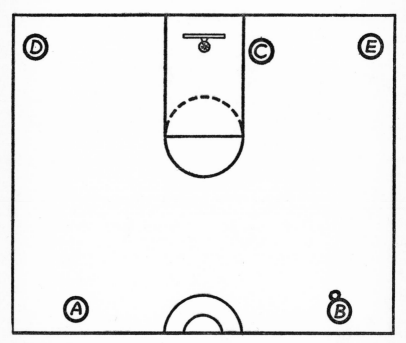

DIAGRAM 17. *The Wide Formation.* We will attack immediately from this wide formation if we have the opponents' outside men beaten down the court or have a one-on-one situation. If these opportunities are not present, our back court players will set up one of our offenses and initiate a play.

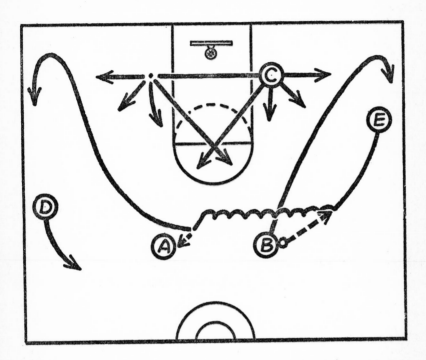

DIAGRAM 18. *The Four-Man Weave.* In our pivot offense we use the weave, chiefly employing a flat corner-to-corner path and going both in front and behind the ball. Whenever we get an opponent beat—we go! We set our pivot plays up from the weave. The plays are determined by the move or moves made by the man with the ball. We do not use finger or number signals. If a player in the back court uses the give-and-go, the pivot man immediately clears out. If a player has his opponent beaten while setting up a play—that is it! He drives! The play is secondary.

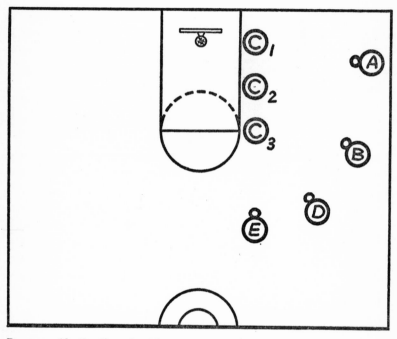

DIAGRAM 19. *Feeding the Pivot.* At Dartmouth, we prefer to feed the pivot player from the side. Player A is in good position to feed C in position 1. B is in good position to feed C in position 2 and D is in a good position to feed C in position 3. With the ball in possession of player E, the pivot player should break out fast from position 1 to position 3.

Pivot Formation

The use of the pivot as a team offense means that the pivot player will be stationed in a position so that he can score, dribble to the basket, or feed cutting teammates. The pivot is not planned for ball protection except as this need arises in the general play of the game. In a post or a double-post attack, the backup player may or may not be the important factor in the offense. However, in the pivot attack, the offense is built around his abilities.

Pivot attacks operate in so many ways that it is impossible to set up all the possibilities. These may comprehend a continuity of players in the various positions. When such a continuity or rotation is used, each attacking player moves to the corner, side, underbasket, or rear-court position in turn and breaks to the ball in setting up plays.

This rotation offense, of course, requires that all players be versed in the use of the post, turn around, scissors, screening, and pivot scoring plays which are included in the pivot attack. The chief advantage of this position continuity is that it permits the attacking players to determine which of the defensive opponents are weak in switching and guarding abilities.

The single pivot attack may be used strictly for scoring, or as a feeding medium for cutting players. When designed to advance the ball into the hands of a pivot player so that he may score, it is difficult to plan plays. The chief offensive difficulty has to do with the maneuvering of the pivot player so that he may secure a position where good shots can be attempted.

Pivot players are usually chosen for underbasket duty because of their height. An increased advantage accompanies height when the player is well proportioned or heavy in build. Defensive guarding has become so efficient that tall, slender players can usually be forced away from the basket and their effectiveness as scorers decreased.

When the pivot player is used as a feeding medium, best results will undoubtedly be secured when he moves toward the ball from a position under the basket or breaks out from the corners.

The close-up pivot man must keep in mind that a scoring play by a teammate can be spoiled if he fails to clear out of the underbasket area. When the pivot player moves away from the play, his respective guard may switch. He should expect this switch and be prepared for a pass from the cutting teammate. (Return pass plays which are designed to provide the pivot player with quick shooting opportunities following a switch should be a planned and a practiced part of the attack.)

Due to the premium today on big men, I think you must have a pivot offense as part of your offensive setup. While we don't believe in spending the whole night in trying to feed the pivot, we do believe that the pivot man should work to get the ball. Years ago, I thought you could do without a pivot offense, but today I think it should be used even if only as a flash or moving pivot.

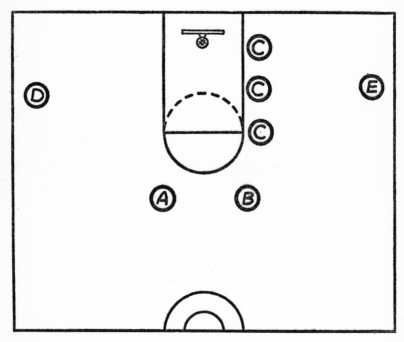

DIAGRAM 20. *Pivot Formation Positions.* Our pivot C takes one of three spots: low, medium, or high outside. A and B are out front while D and E operate on the sidelines (not too deep in the corners).

In starting our circulation in the pivot set-up, we use a weave, moving in front or behind the ball (always watching our pivot player C). C moves with the ball and should be in a position to receive it at any time. While the players are using the weave they keep three things in mind:

1. The give-and-go
2. The screen to the ball
3. The screen away from the ball
   a. Go without the ball
   b. Keep moving
   c. Do not go too fast

Each player must be sure to see the type of move made by the man who passed the ball. This takes only a fraction of a second and, to a great extent, determines the play.

THREE-TWO OFFENSE

The Three-Two Offense circulation resembles that used in the five-man weave. In the Three-Two, the two corner players may be used as "flash" pivot men or operate "in the hole" from time to time as the "big man." The corner men can get good positions by cutting across the lane from one side of the court to the other. In the weave, they are expected to work in the back court and help out with defensive balance. The back court players use the give-and-go, moving and set screens, slicing plays, and dribble and post-and-pivot screens to free teammates for a scoring play. Good plays will result from the ball-ahead-of-the-man principle. Five-man weave plays also blend into this offense and help to maintain offensive and defensive balance.

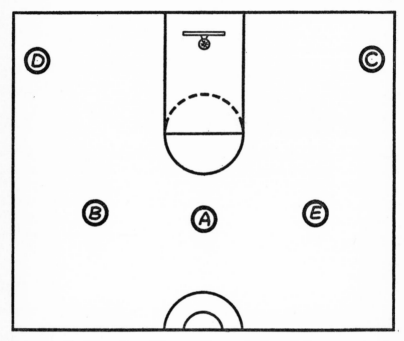

DIAGRAM 21. *Three-Two Offense.* Players A, B and E operate in the back court, using screens and give-and-go principles to set up plays with the corner men (D and C).

5

Formation Principles and Plays

I once heard one coach say to another: "I want to give you a couple of good plays." The other coach said: "Give me a couple of good players and forget the plays." How true!

We use only four or five plays in our man-to-man offense. All other plays are free lance in nature. We do not like to put "handcuffs" on a player by saying he must do this or do that. . . . We especially want to capitalize on a player's natural ability and the skills in which he excels.

Again, basically, we do certain things in our offense which we feel will help *every* player. We predicate our system on three principles:

1. The give-and-go
2. The screen to the ball
3. The screen away from the ball

If these three principles are observed, we believe our players will be able to play good basketball. Such moves as driving without the ball; learning to screen between, in front, and back of the ball; and to blend in with the plays, are important and become a part of the three principles listed above.

Now, for the plays we use in the various formations. Naturally, they are used on the left as well as on the right side of the court, although only one side will be shown in the diagrams.

Pivot Formation Plays: In the pivot formation all players

except the pivot man are moving from one position to another and interchanging so that each may have an opportunity to feed, cut, dribble, or attempt a shot. The purpose of this attack is to determine which of our opponents are most susceptible to the various plays which are possible. All players must be well versed in the requirements of the various positions. Because there are no definite position assignments, this type of attack requires an experienced all-around squad. We try to set up the three-man triangle formation when using the pivot formation.

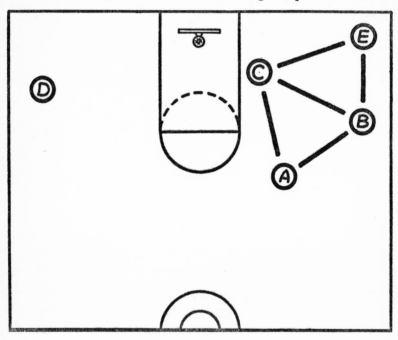

DIAGRAM 22. *Three-Man Triangles.* Here, A, B and E with the co-operation of C set up triangles.

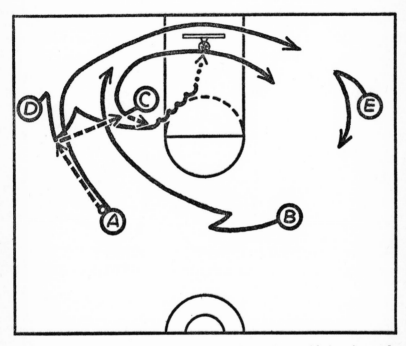

DIAGRAM 23. *Running Screen Play.* Our players know this is going to be a running screen play because A makes a base line clear-out after passing the ball to D. D, here, passed to C and cut as shown. C returns the ball to D if he breaks free. B cuts as shown and E will cover the backcourt.

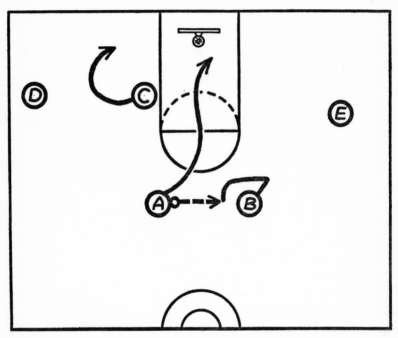

DIAGRAM 24. *Give-and-Go Play.* Player A is starting a give-and-go play with B, and the pivot player (C) clears out so the free-throw lane will not be clogged up.

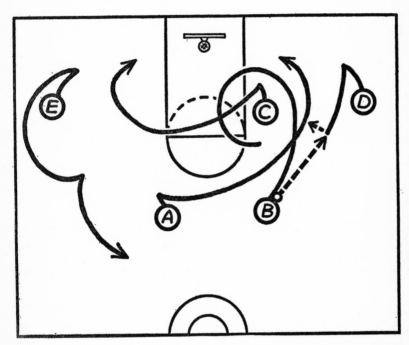

DIAGRAM 25. *Running Screen Play.* B passes to D, cuts between D and his defensive opponent, and comes slowly out to the spot where the free-throw line meets the lane. Now, A makes a fake to go left and then cuts off C, getting a delayed pass from D. As the base line is being cleared by B, C goes to the other side of the lane and, with his hand up, looks for a pass from A. E pulls out to the back court. Note that we have everything going one way, making the switch by the defense more difficult than normally. (See variation which follows.)

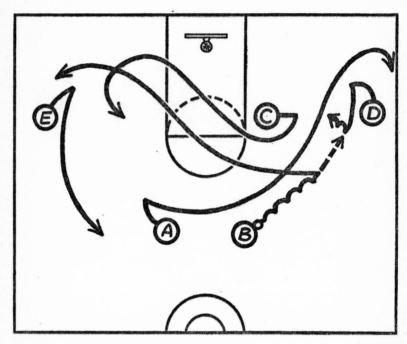

DIAGRAM 26. *Side Give-and-Go.* This play differs from the previous running screen play in that B, instead of circling back to the free-throw line, tries a "side" give-and-go.

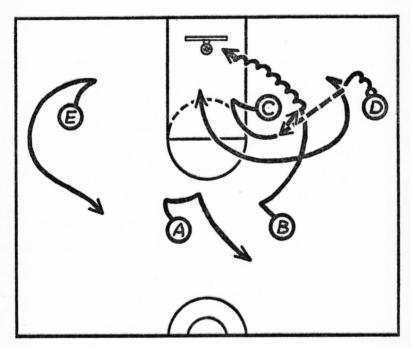

DIAGRAM 27. *Counter for Sagging Defense.* As soon as we get the triangle set up with B, C, and D or, on the other side, A, C, and E, we
try to split the post. In the above, D hits C and cuts as shown. Then,
B fakes a drive and cuts off D's tail as quickly and closely as possible.
If done properly, this play forces the opponents into a double switch.

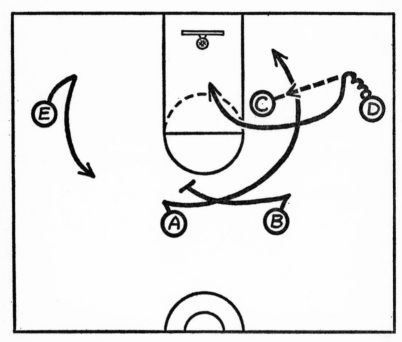

DIAGRAM 28. *Variation of Counter for Sagging Defense.*   In this, B screens for A instead of cutting through. You will notice that on this play as well as in the preceding play, one whole side of the floor has been cleared out.

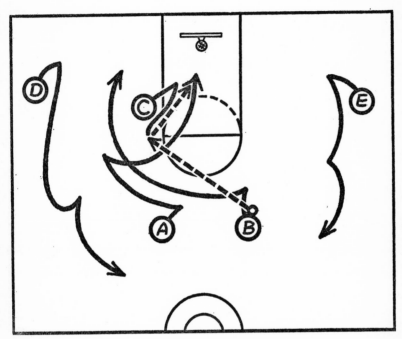

DIAGRAM 29. *Trailer Scissors.* On this play we want our pivot high but outside the lane. If B can feed C, he does so and cuts as shown. Now note A starts his cut on the same side to which B is cutting. When A gets opposite C he changes direction and cuts to the other side. We feel that this is a better play than the ordinary criss-cross which splits the post.

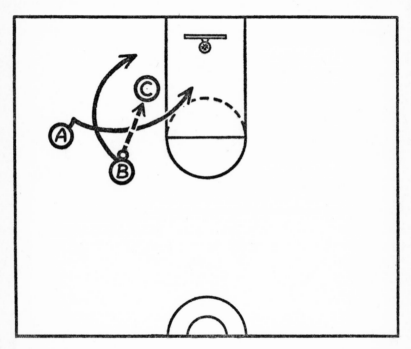

Diagram 30. *Straight Criss-Cross.* This is an easy play for the opponents to defend with a slide or a switch. It shows all the way and we do not bother to use it.

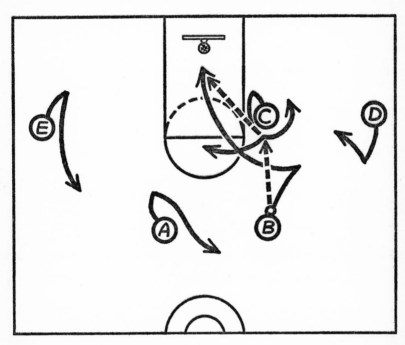

DIAGRAM 31. *The Simple Simon.* Simple? Yes but effective! B hits C on the move and starts to cut to the outside. B does not take his defensive opponent deep into the post but cuts inside after a step or two. The defense players expect the outside drive and overplay their offense opponents. That is the reason the play as shown above is successful. After C hits B, he rolls toward the basket (left or right) and may receive a return pass.

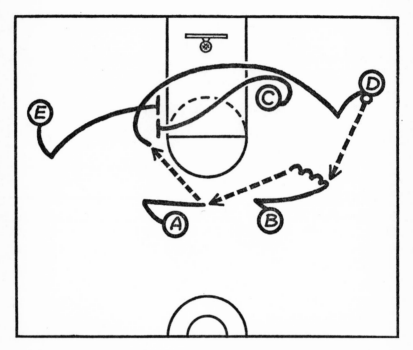

DIAGRAM 32. *The Double Screen*. B fakes a screen toward D and receives the ball. E takes a position on the free-throw lane. C fakes a cut
and sets up a double-screen with E. B hits A. When D cuts around the
double screen, A hits him with the ball.

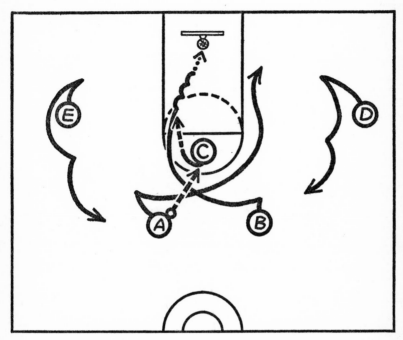

DIAGRAM 33. *High Post Play.* A hits C on the high post and cuts as shown. B cuts hard and fast off the tail of A. C waits for the second cutter to get by, then turns around, faces the basket, and gives B the ball with a delayed pass. (C can keep, shoot or drive.)

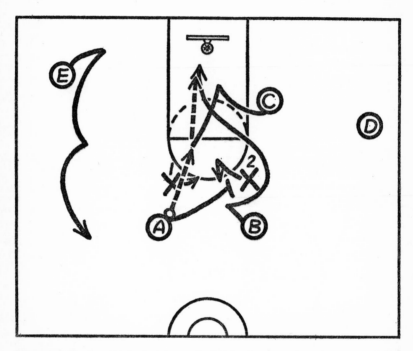

DIAGRAM 34. *St. Michaels Play.* St. Michaels uses this play successfully. Offensive player A hits C on the high post. A and B then move as if to execute a split. The defensive players, X-1 and X-2, may or may not execute a switch. A starts his cut and stops about a foot short of the high post, slightly to the right. B starts to cut as if executing a criss-cross but does a "shake" and continues his cut on the right side. The slight change of direction made by B usually enables him to get inside the defensive player on his drive to the basket. C passes to B.

THREE-TWO FORMATION PLAYS

Most any play which is run from the Pivot Offense can be run from the Three-Two Offense. In fact, some plays set up better. We have been using this offense for years and use it mainly as a change of pace. We have found that after an opposing team has played for a time against your pivot offense, the use of the Three-Two Offense as a change will help the entire campaign. Another important factor regarding the Three-Two is that it is a good ball-handling formation and is a great help in developing the pivot players.

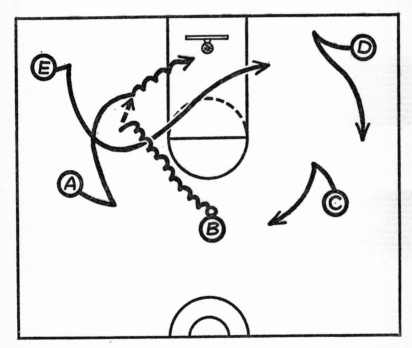

DIAGRAM 35. *Dribble-Pivot Play.* B dribbles as if to drive. He stops when he gets near the free-throw line and turns his back to the basket. E fakes and cuts first. A cuts off the tail of E. D pulls out and C moves over.

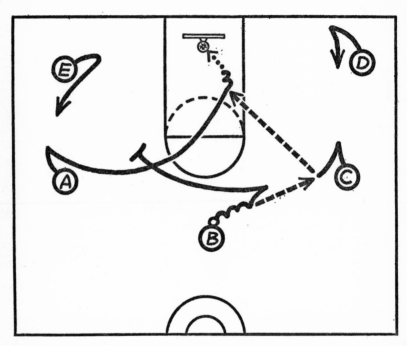

DIAGRAM 36. *Push give-and-go play.*   B passes to C and screens away for A. A fakes left and uses B's screen for a long cut to the basket. If A breaks free, C passes the ball to him.

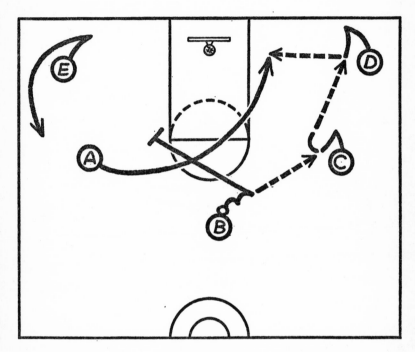

DIAGRAM 37. *Variation 1 (Push Give-and-Go)*. B passes to C, uses the "V" and screens for A. This time, however, C passes to D. D passes to A. E pulls out.

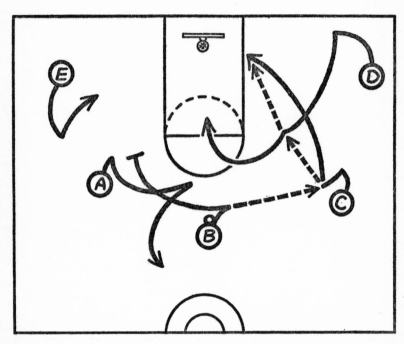

DIAGRAM 38. *Variation 2 (Push Give-and-Go)*. This is to take care of the switch. B passes to C and screens away. As soon as a defense player calls "switch," A executes a "V" or clears out. D comes into the pivot and C and D use the "Two-on-Two" in passing-off, keeping, or splitting. E follows in.

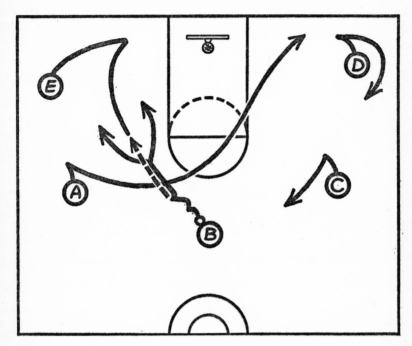

DIAGRAM 39. *Open-up Play.* We call this "opening up the floor." (A) goes without the ball to opposite corner. E immediately moves into pivot, and B and E play "two-on-two." C covers the ball and D pulls out.

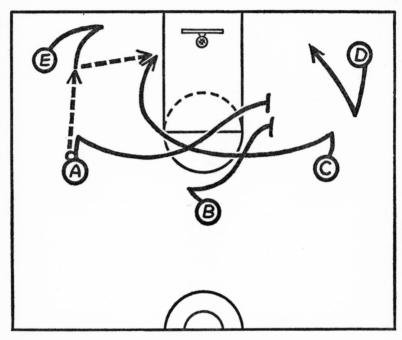

DIAGRAM 40. *Double-Screen Play.*   (A) passes to E and cuts to the opposite side of the free-throw lane. There he is joined by B who aids him in setting up a double screen. C delays and then cuts around the double screen and drives for the basket. E passes the ball to him if he breaks free.

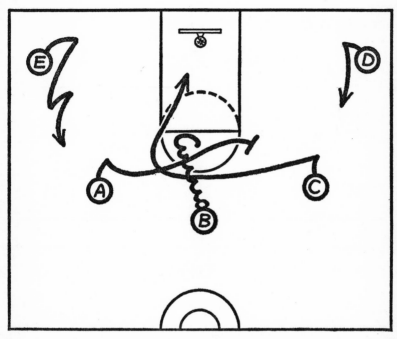

DIAGRAM 41. *Dribble-Screen Plays.* Remember that we set up all plays while on the move. We do not set up from a standing formation. If we can get a "one-on-one" or a "two-on-two" situation, we take it. In fact, whenever we have the defense beat, we *go!* In the above diagram, B dribbles to a high post and pivots. From this situation we run all our high-post plays.

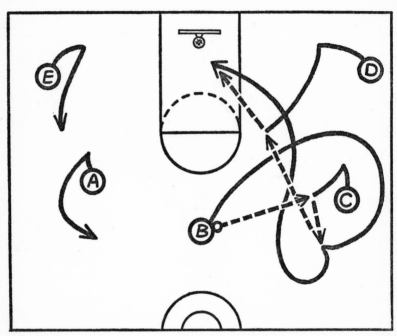

DIAGRAM 42. *Back Run-Around.* B passes to C, screens C's opponent, and runs around in back of C. C gives him an over-the-shoulder pass. D moves into pivot. B passes to D. C cuts first and then B cuts. C can cut either side. B goes to the opposite side. E pulls out and A goes over. (This is a little French Pastry to keep the defense moving.)

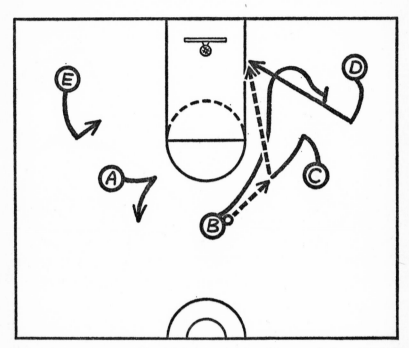

DIAGRAM 43. *Corner Pick.* This is a simple pick out of the corner. B passes to C and sets a screen in the right corner behind D's opponent. C fakes a return pass to B and then sets for a shot. When D drives around B's screen, C passes the ball to him. (This play can also come to the first, second, or third man out of the corner in our regular weave offense.)

ADDITIONAL THREE-TWO OFFENSE PLAYS

At Dartmouth we use the following plays for general practice to familiarize our players with the possibilities of our Three-Two Offense.

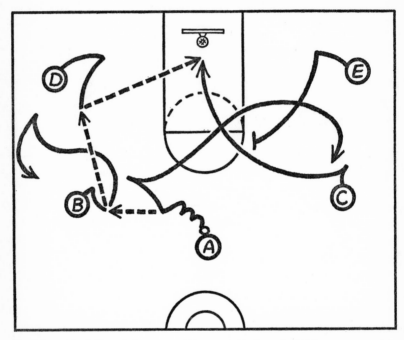

DIAGRAM 44. *"V" and Screen.*   (A) passes to B and "V's" away to screen for C. B passes the ball to D who has faked along the baseline and cut out to meet the pass. B follows his pass as shown. E cuts out to a position on the free-throw line to set up a set screen for C. D passes the ball to C if he succeeds in breaking loose.

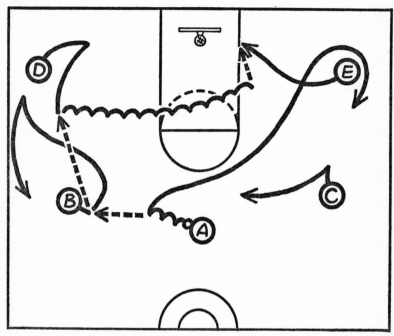

DIAGRAM 45. *Dribble, "V" and Screen.* (A) dribbles to the left and passes to B. Then he screens down and across for E in the corner. B passes to D and follows his pass. D dribbles to a pivot position and E cuts past him and receives the ball for a shot if he is free.

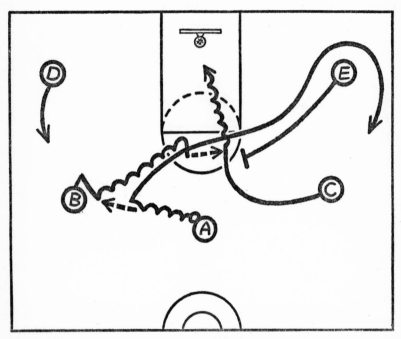

DIAGRAM 46. *Dribble and "V."*   (A) dribbles to the left and passes to B. (A) now "V's" away and again screens for E. This time, B dribbles to a position on the free-throw line and hands-off to C who has cut through the free-throw lane around the block set by E.

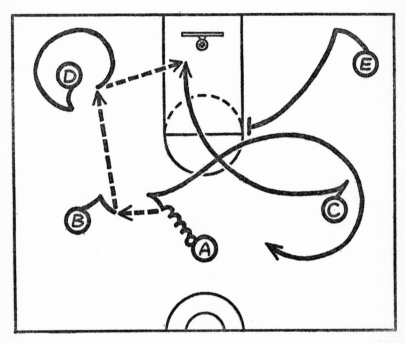

DIAGRAM 47. *Dribble and "V" and Double Screen.* (A) dribbles to the left, passes to B, and "V's" away to set a screen for C on the free-throw line. B passes to D. Corner man E establishes a set screen beside the lane. C drives his opponent straight toward the baseline and then changes direction and cuts to the left and down the lane. D passes the ball to C for the shot.

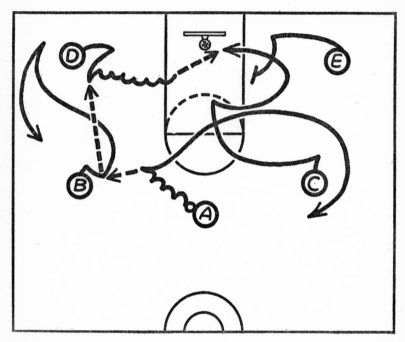

DIAGRAM 48. *Dribble, "V" and Screen.* (A) again dribbles to the left, passes to B, and "V's" away. B passes to D and follows his pass. D dribbles across the lane to a pivot position. E drives to the baseline and then reverses back to a position beside the lane. Player C drives hard for the free-throw lane, reverses and cuts around E.

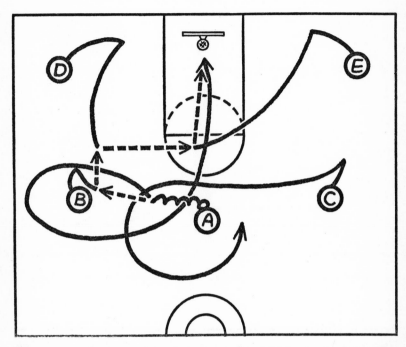

DIAGRAM 49. *Dribble and Back Screen.*   (A) dribbles to the left, passes
to B, and screens for him. D drives toward the baseline and then breaks
out for the pass from B. E breaks to the free-throw line and receives the
ball from D. (A) continues on around B and cuts through the free-throw
lane and receives the ball from E for a shot.

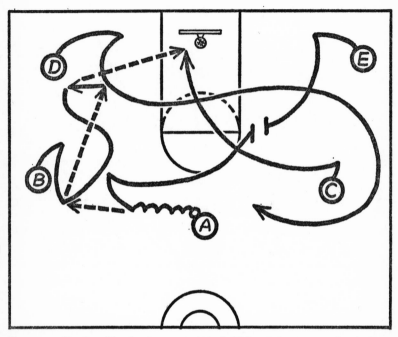

DIAGRAM 50. *Double Set-Screen.* (A) dribbles left, passes the ball to
B, "V's" away, and sets a screen at the free-throw-line. B passes to D and
follows the pass. D returns the ball to B and cuts across the lane. E
breaks out beside the lane and sets a screen beside A forming a double
screen. C cuts down the lane inside A and E and receives the ball from B.

6

The Dartmouth Offense
Auxiliary

We teach offense formations for the auxiliary situations after our basic defense and offense principles have been thoroughly mastered. However, it is unwise to wait too long to teach the offensive and defensive tactics to be used in the auxiliary situations. The ability to set up the formation, give the proper signal, get the ball and execute a play is an important team asset. A team which sets up its auxiliary formations quickly and surely has an effect upon the opponents which makes them defense conscious. Further, it accentuates the fact that the team has been well coached.

Most teams get worried when opposing a team which sets up a formation in a business-like and confident manner. At Dartmouth, we do not plan and practice held-ball plays as such. We concentrate on gaining possession of the ball and letting our players go on from there in making a play. Naturally, we have a number of out-of-bounds plays which we practice and use in given situations. It is important that your best out-of-bounds play be kept under wraps until a "clutch" basket might be scored from an out-of-bounds situation.

Held-ball and out-of-bounds situations vary in number during any given game but it is extremely wise to be ready, to have your team equipped to take care of the situation promptly and efficiently. Possession is the thing! Getting the tap and losing the ball are unforgivable. Just as bad or worse is the loss of the ball from a throw-in from out-of-bounds. The fact that a team has a formation and moves to protect the tap or throw-in is some insurance against these interceptions.

HELD BALL PLAYS

Possession of the ball from held-ball situations is more important today than at any time in the history of basketball. Therefore, we devote a lot of time to jumping practice and to held-ball situations. In pre-season practice we spend much time in teaching jumping. Separating the players into groups of three, one man tosses, two jump, and each group rotates assignments. Like all clubs, we have an offensive and a defensive held-ball set-up.

On all taps we use the words: "Ours" or "Theirs." We line up in three different formations—the box—the diamond—and the wide diamond. We never use the "T" when the jump is the opponents' (theirs). If the opponents have the tall or best leaper, we use the term "theirs" and use our defensive formation. However, *this does not mean that we concede the ball.*

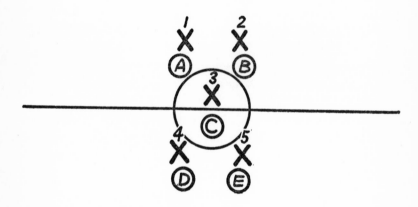

DIAGRAM 51. *The Box Formation.* Back Tap. Our guards, D and E, permit their opponents to move in front of them and get good blocking positions. The tap from C is straight back and the forwards, A and B, are expected to secure the ball.

DIAGRAM 52. *The Wide Diamond Formation.* If D is unguarded, we tap to him. However, an opponent usually plays him, even if D moves clear to the sideline. When this happens, E moves up to the left or right of opponent 5 and we are able to get two of our players next to each other. We then tap the ball between them. Player E must take care of the defense as soon as the ball is tapped.

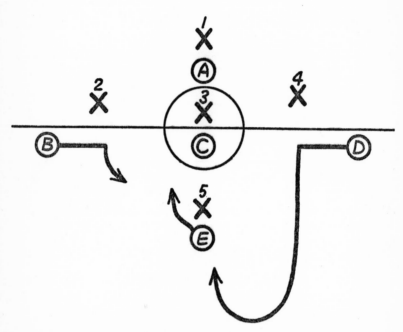

DIAGRAM 53. *Tap from Wide Diamond.* Here, the tap is made between B and E because they have moved next to each other. Teammate D breaks toward the center and then drops back for safety.

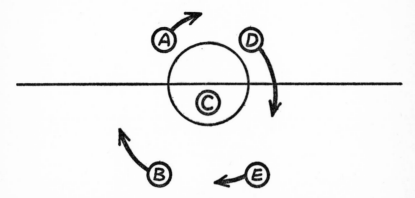

DIAGRAM 54. *Moving into the "T" Tap Formation.* When we feel the opponents have the edge in height or jumping ability, we move into our "T" formation. (Only on center circle taps.) See next diagram.

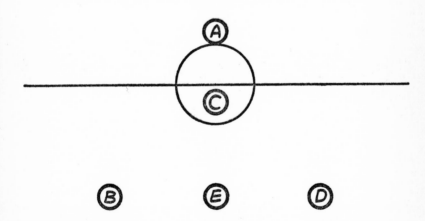

DIAGRAM 55. *Defensive "T" for Center-Jump.* From the box formation in the previous diagram, we moved into the safety "T" shown above.

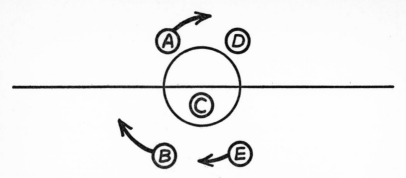

DIAGRAM 56. *Rotating Principle.* If we think we have a chance to "steal" the ball when the opponents control the tap we use our rotating principle (moving right or left on signal). This revolving always ends up in a defensive position since we are using it because we feel the opposing jumper is superior to ours.

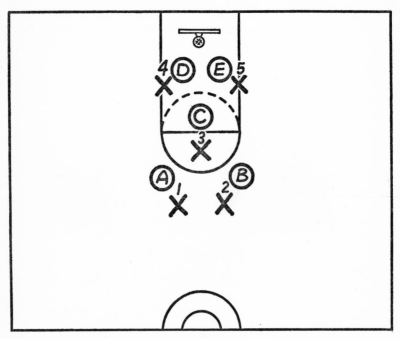

DIAGRAM 57. *Held-Ball at Defensive Basket.* (Usual held-ball formation). On this set-up you will note that we always take the *inside* positions toward the basket. This forces the opponents to go around us. Players D and E play a little closer together so opponents 4 and 5 cannot receive the ball and swing "in" for a shot.

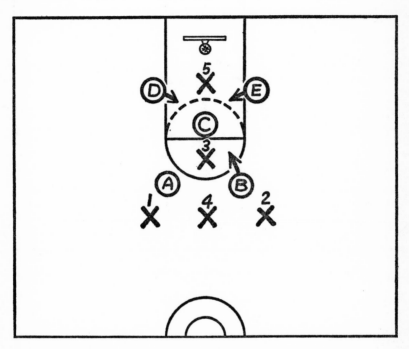

DIAGRAM 58. *Opponents in One-One-Three Held-Ball Formation.* If our opponents take this formation, we will tap the ball between A and D or between B and E. If the opponents set up any other formation, we will try to set up so that two of our players are next to one another and tap the ball between them. (A defensive movement must always be made when under the defensive basket.)

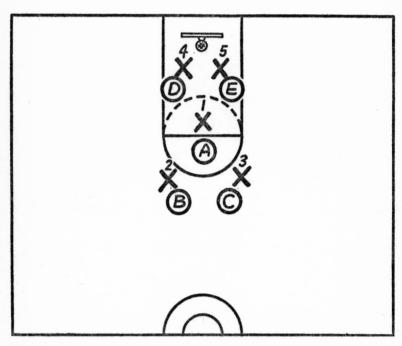

DIAGRAM 59. *Held-Ball at Offensive Basket. Our Tap.*   Tap will be made between B and C if opponents 2 and 3 play tight as shown above. A forward tap will be made to the outside of D or E.

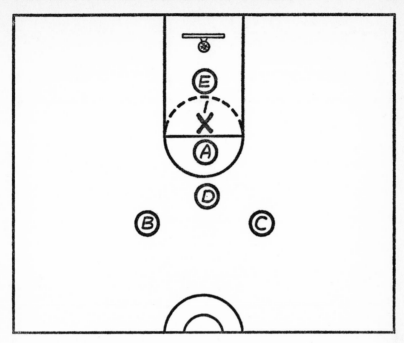

DIAGRAM 60. *Held-Ball at Offensive Basket. Their Tap.* We *immediately* go into our "T" formation so the opponents will not use the tap and the long cut to beat us back to their basket. We take no chances in this situation.

OUT-OF-BOUNDS PLAYS

Probably no more than one formation should be practiced for front and back court use. Two or three plays for the front court can be developed, but possession may be sufficient in the back court. (Fast-break methods may be used following possession of the ball in the back court.) These plays work on both sides of the court:

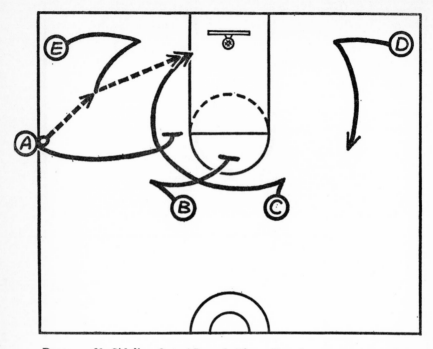

Diagram 61. *Sideline Out-of-Bounds Play.* You do not get many of these in a game and they seldom work. However, they do serve to protect the ball and proper execution and defensive sluggishness might result in a score.

Player A has ball out of bounds. E fakes a cut for the basket and breaks out toward the ball. (A) passes to E (short pass) and B screens for C. As soon as A passes to E, he cuts directly toward the free-throw line and, with B, sets up a double screen. C cuts around the double screen and gets the ball from E. There are several variations on this play, but side line situations between the center line and the base line come up so seldom that it would be a waste of space to diagram them.

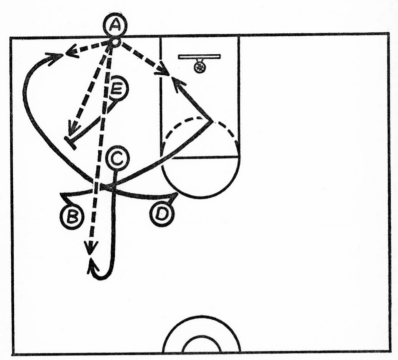

DIAGRAM 62. *Clair Bee Out-of-Bounds Play.* I got this base line out-of-bounds play and the variations which follow from Clair Bee. They have been highly successful and we use them in every game. When the man with the ball (A) gives the starting signal (slapping the ball, calling a number, etc.), teammate E, facing the ball, moves back and teammate D cuts close behind him and on to the corner. Player B fakes left, waits for D to clear and then cuts as shown above. He (B) is the first pass choice. Note that B changes direction in the lane and cuts toward the ball. Alternate passes follow in the order of preference to E, D and C. Player C holds his set screen until D and B have cleared and then drops back for the safety pass.

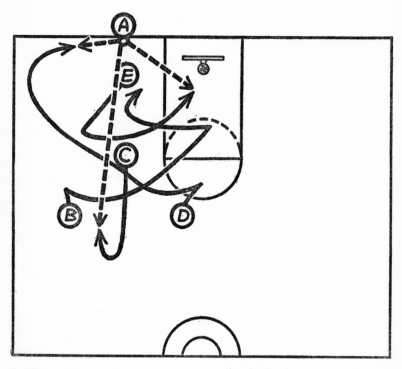

DIAGRAM 63. *Variation #1, Clair Bee Out-of-Bounds Play.* This play starts as in the basic play. Here, however, instead of continuing on to the ball, player B throws a hard stop in the lane and then uses a "V" to set up a double screen with C. Player E swings around and cuts between B and C and receives the ball from A in front of the basket (bounce pass). After E has cut in front of him, C drops back for a safety pass. All players move quickly and surely. The pass sequence from A to his teammates is as follows: E, D, B, C.

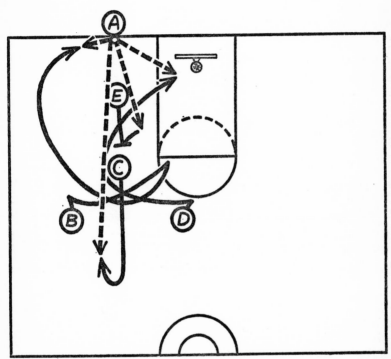

DIAGRAM 64. *Variation #2, Clair Bee Out-of-Bounds Play.* Here, the play is set up for player D. Teammate E drops straight back behind C's opponent. D starts as in the previous plays. Now, however, instead of continuing on to the corner, he circles around C and E and toward the basket. Should E's opponent switch to cover D, the ball is passed to E for a jump shot. Note that B has reversed and cut back to the corner position. The order of passes: D, E, B and C (safety pass).

7

Attacking the
Zone Defenses

At Dartmouth we feel that the effectiveness of the zone defense is determined not so much by the formation (player alignment) as by the aggressiveness and determination of the zone players. For that reason we employ but one alignment to attack all zones—the One-Three-One.

The One-Three-One attack sets up with a single player (the quarterback) in the back court, and a good ballhandler in near the free-throw line. Then two cutters (wing men) who are good shooters on each side of the court in line with the post player, and an aggressive follow-in board man who works along the base line and under the basket.

The back court player controls the ball and sets up the plays. He should be a good passer, dribbler and shooter. He is in charge of offense and is responsible for the team's defensive balance.

The middle player should be tall, have hand-off ability, be a good shot from the free-throw line area, and have follow-in power.

The wing men must be able to score. They should be able to shoot from the sides and corners, possess good jump shots, be able to dribble in for a score and feed the pivot.

The base line player must be strong, tall, and able to score near the basket. He should have a good corner shot and the knack of scoring tip-in shots under the basket.

The One-Three-One attack is designed to spread the zone defense, although it is possible to overload on one side of the court through movement. We like to use the jump shot from near the free-throw circle, where it is an important scoring weapon. Keep in mind that the Dartmouth attack against any type of zone emphasizes movement. We do not just stand around passing the ball from one man to another until someone decides to take a shot!

We try to move so that the opponents can at no time definitely determine the positions of our players. We don't want the opponents to use their zone against us in the same manner they practice it, and our drives and moves are designed to force our opponents to make some sort of a new slide or maneuver. Further, we feel that a few lay-up shots will upset our opponents. We constantly try for them.

Patience: We repeat this word again and again. "Be patient! Drive and pass and fill the vacant zone openings and you will get a good shot. The size of the score is not important as long as you have the most points. You can't do better than win!"

A zone offense, which limits areas of attack to its players, is playing into the hands of the opponents. If an offensive player remains in one area as a part of a set formation, the zone player's job becomes simple. However, if the attack shifts and moves its players and the ball, the zone defense cannot remain static. The zone players must move and change direction and hustle back and forth to stop openings. And, eventually, because of all these moves and shifts, one of the zone players will make a mistake. This is where "patience" comes through. It must be sold to the attacking players and developed by drill work in attacking the various zones.

ZONE ATTACK PRINCIPLES

We attack all zones with practically the same offense. We will move against the zone, driving with and without the ball. Basically, we will try at all times to drive past the front or side men, forcing one of the back line men to pick up the driver. If we are successful in this maneuver, we will then send one of

our men to the spot left vacant by the opponent who covers
the driver. The ball will be passed to this teammate as quickly
as possible for a shot or a pass.

In our standard zone attack formation, we try to set up the
One-Three-One and then move to positions which will set up
triangles from which to start our passing and cutting. See
diagram which follows.

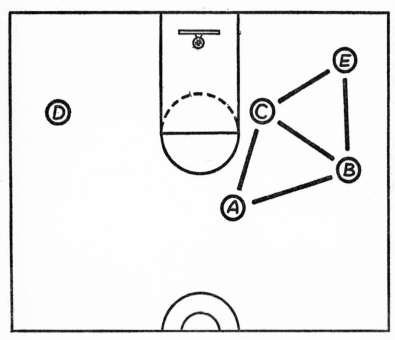

DIAGRAM 65. *Setting up Triangles.* A, B and E have moved to positions
which permit passing and cutting from triangles. C must maneuver for
good pass positions.

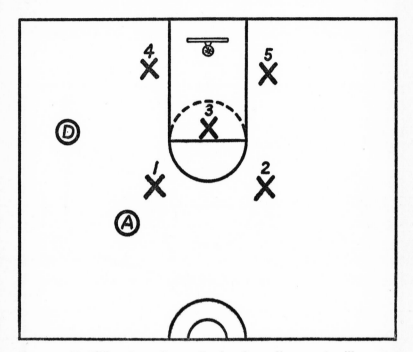

DIAGRAM 66. *Filling Open Spots.* In the above diagram, A will attempt to drive past defensive 1. Should defensive X-3 or X-4 cover him, we will send men to the spots left open. (See following diagram.) "Go where they ain't!"

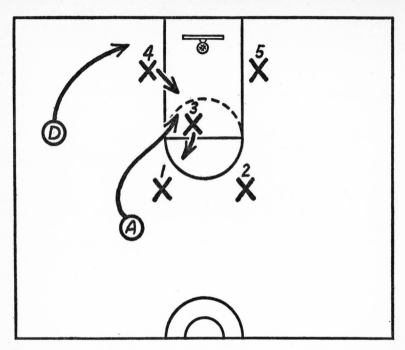

DIAGRAM 67. *Filling Open Spots* (Continued).   Here, offensive player A drove past defense chaser X-1 and into defense player X-3's territory. In the above diagram, defense player X-4 moves to the lane to assist defense player X-3. Offense player D immediately cuts into the territory left vacant by defensive X-4.

The above is just one example of our zone attack cutting principle, but we try to do this on any move which will result in a zone defensive man leaving his area. In other words, in opposing a zone we use directly opposite methods from those we use in attacking the man-to-man defense. When driving against a zone, we tell our men to go to the open spots and *toward* our driver. We keep at this constantly, looking for the defensive slide which will leave a vacant zone or area. Now, for a few of our plays against the zone. (Keep in mind that these plays work on both sides of the court.)

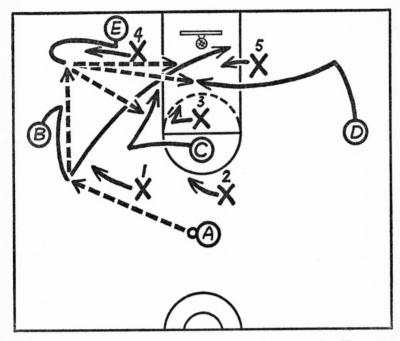

DIAGRAM 68. *Basic Zone Attack Alignment.* The Two-One-Two zone defense formation is being attacked here by our basic One-Three-One attack. Player A passes to B because we have a base line man on that side (E). As the pass is being made, E moves out along the base line and gets a pass from B. Now, B cuts for the basket and, if open, E will pass to him. If B does not get the ball he takes a position on the other side of the basket. As soon as B cuts, C will cut right off his tail. If C is open, E will pass the ball to him. Offensive player D now times his move and cuts into the center of the lane near the free-throw line. E has the option of passing to B, C, or D. If E gets into trouble, he dribbles out so he can pass to A. Then we start all over again on either side. And—we keep moving.

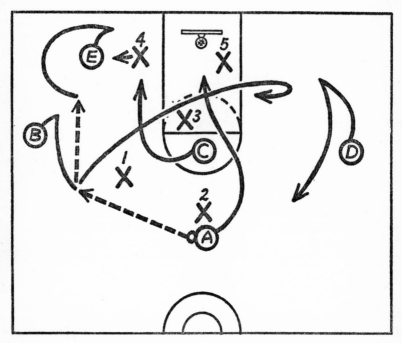

DIAGRAM 69. *Variation #1, Basic Zone Attack.*   Players A and D change positions (assignments). While this may seem like only one play, it is a continuity offense with options. If we can drive at any time with the ball from any position, we will do so.

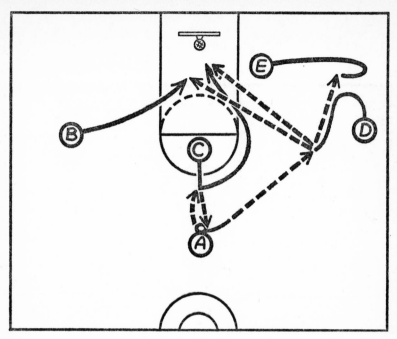

DIAGRAM 70. *Variation #2, Basic Zone Attack.* The above diagram shows the set-up on the right side of the court. Here, we show slight variation in the play of C which may be necessary when it is difficult to pass to the high post. We call this our beep-beep play. C will come out to within an arm's length of A and A will give him the ball. C will pass it right back. As soon as he passes the ball back to A, C drives for the basket at full speed on D's side of the lane. (A) passed the ball to D as soon as he received it back from C, and E pulls out from the basket and along the base line at the same time. If a defensive opponent does not play C, D hits him with the ball. If C does not receive the ball, he continues on to the other side of the basket. D now passes to E on the base line or to B cutting from the weak side to the free-throw lane. Naturally, if left with the ball, D or E may drive to the basket, or they may shoot.

The following diagrams show our One-Three-One attack opposed to a One-Two-Two zone defense.

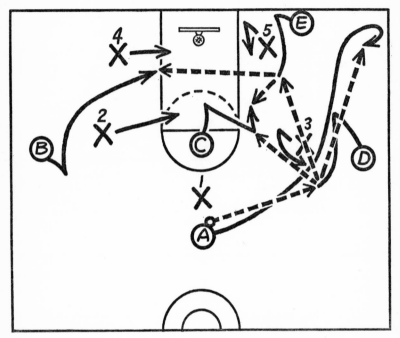

DIAGRAM 71. *Attacking the One-Two-Two Zone.* (A) passes to D and cuts past defensive player X-3. If X-3 does not defense A, D will pass the ball to him for a jump shot. If this pass is not made, D will have the option of passing to C or E. Should X-5 fail to cover A in the corner, D may pass to him for a corner shot. Should X-5 cover A in the corner, D may pass to E for a shot near the basket. Should X-4 cover him, E may pass to C beside the lane or to B who is cutting for the basket.

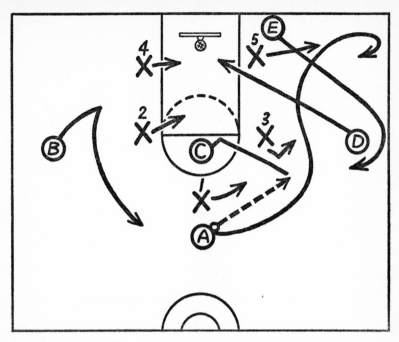

DIAGRAM 72. *Attacking the One-Two-Two Zone* (Continued). The post player (C) breaks out to the side and receives the ball from A. (A) cuts past C and on to the corner. D delays and then cuts for the basket. B replaces (A) in the back court. C faces the basket as soon as he gets the ball and attempts a shot if not covered by X-3. Post man C can pass to D, E, or to A in the corner if covered by X-3.

Attacking the Three-Two Zone. Although we seldom meet the Three-Two zone, our players attack it with the One-Three-One as they do all zone defenses. We oppose all types of zones during our practice sessions so we will be familiar with the moves against the different alignments and positions.

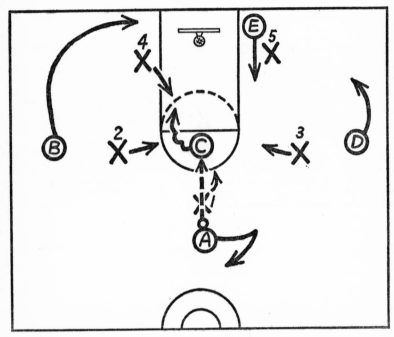

DIAGRAM 73. *Attacking the Three-Two Zone.* The Three-Two Zone is weak in the middle (free-throw area) and we center our attack there. In the diagram above, offensive player A passes to C. Now that we have the ball past the defensive front line, we quickly focus our attack on defensive players X-4 and X-5. The post player (C) turns quickly toward the basket. If unguarded he will shoot (one-hand set). Should X-2 or X-3 rush him, he will use his jump shot. If C cannot get a good shot away, he will dribble toward the basket (either side). If X-5 meets him, C will pass to E. Should X-4 oppose him, he will pass to B cuttting under the basket. Teammate D will nearly always be free on the base line on the right side or in the right corner.

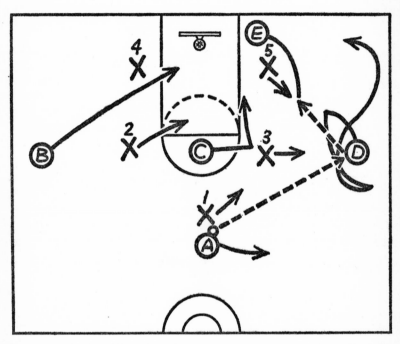

DIAGRAM 74. *Attacking the Three-Two Zone* (Continued). When defensive players X-2 and X-4 tighten up toward C on the post, D drives a short distance, "V's" back and receives the ball from A. Teammate E now breaks out to the ball. B fills the spot left open by E and E has the option of shooting, passing to C along the lane to the basket, to B under the basket, or to D in the right corner.

8

Offensive Counters for Special Situations

All teams should have offensive maneuvers for special situations. Once we recognize an opponent's defensive strategy we try to counter with an offensive move. But, long before we encounter most of the usual special situations, we have practiced the counter move which we feel will be most effective. We will touch on these situations from time to time so that the counter will be at our fingertips. Once in a while we are lucky enough to improvise right on the floor during a game.

POSSESSION ATTACK

Possession. If we are trying to hold on to the ball when we are ahead, we use either the semi-freeze or our possession attack. In either case, we are looking for the easy one.

THE FREEZE

The Dartmouth freeze is operated on the same principle which covers our possession attack. However, if we are fortunate and have an expert dribbler, we let him control the ball as much as possible. But we still keep the middle open and we are not looking for the shot as much in the freeze as we are in the possession attack. In either case, we work from the base line out. Cutting is always in and out, out and in, never across court. We *never,* I repeat *never,* cross-screen as shown below.

116

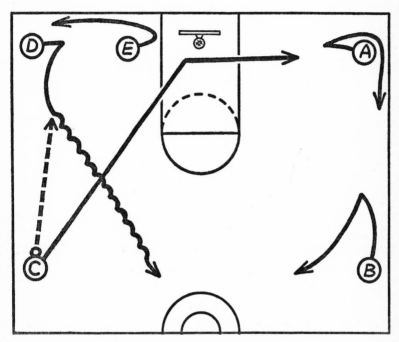

DIAGRAM 75. *Possession Attack Formation.* Player A or D may fake to come up along the sideline and then cut for the basket if an opponent should overshift. Should A or D cut for the basket, the respective corner position would be replaced by a teammate. Note that we keep close to the sidelines in order to make a big court. C passes to D who is advancing up the sideline and then cuts for the basket. Player E now replaces D in the left corner and then advances up the sideline toward D. Any player who reaches one of the backcourt positions (occupied by C and B in the above diagram) may dribble to the other side of the court and start the same procedure.

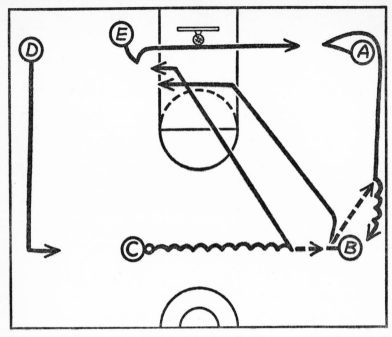

DIAGRAM 76. *Possession Attack* (Continued). In our possession attack we never cross-screen. Further, unless a cutter is wide open, we *never* take a chance on passing the ball to him.

DIAGRAM 77. *Double-Teaming.* Note that defensive players X-1 and X-2 are in excellent positions to double-team offensive player B simply because offensive player A has cross-screened.

ONE-SHOT PLAY

The one-shot play is an important "team" weapon and it is wise to have the play well drilled so that the players will know their assignments. Further, the philosophy upon which the play is based should be understood. When the score is tied and the clock is running out, the team in possession of the ball must decide whether or not it is advisable to hold the ball for one shot. If the shot is taken too soon and missed, the opponents may get the ball and be successful in their scoring attempt and win the game. Most coaches like to hold the ball until there are only seven or eight seconds left before getting set for the "last" shot. Remember, the play works on both sides of the court.

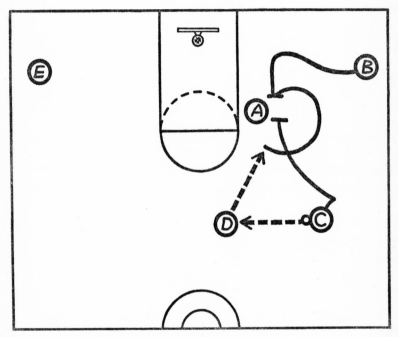

DIAGRAM 78. *A Shot from Scrimmage.* Player B comes out of the corner and stands right beside A (as close as possible). Player C passes to D and moves forward to take B's place beside A. This provides a double screen and B cuts around and out and receives the ball from D. B may now drive, or preferably, shoot. (For our driving plays on the last shot we set up any of our basic plays and designate the shooter.)

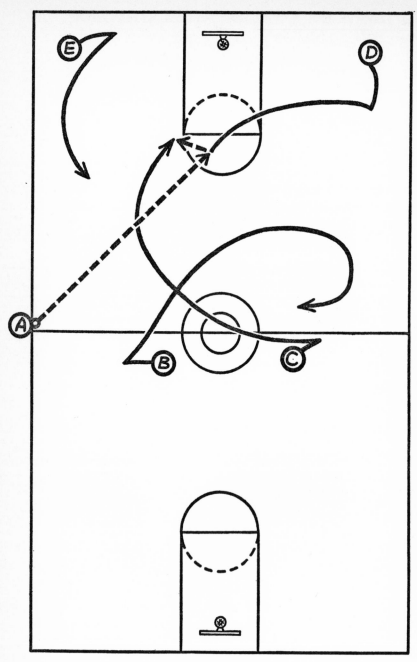

DIAGRAM 79. *A Shot from an Out-of-bounds Situation.* (A) hits D with a high pass coming to the high post position on the move. This play needs timing. B screens for C who cuts. Corner player D can shoot (jump shot) or hand off to C. Player E will follow-in. (We keep it simple.)

Coming Out of the Man-to-Man Press

We usually rely upon one standard formation and series of plays to come out of a press. Further, we are often criticized for having so many men in the back court. However, we have been successful with it and see no reason to change. The important thing to remember about a press is *not* to get *excited*. In fact, about all that concerns your players is to advance your regular offense from the back court instead of the front court. Next in importance is to get the ball across the 10-second line; scoring is secondary.

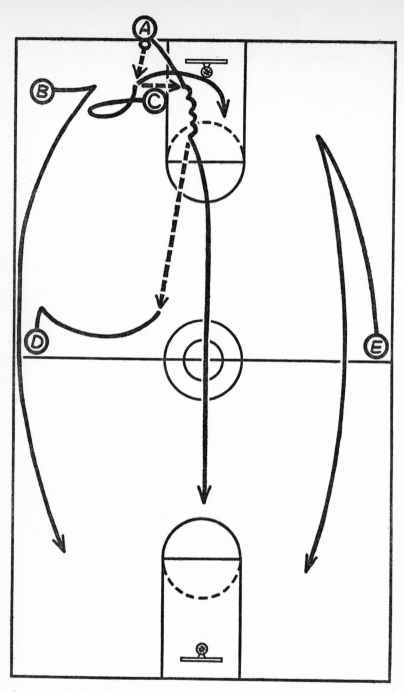

DIAGRAM 80. *Coming out of the Man-to-man Press.* (A) passes to C and breaks up court as shown. C returns the ball to A who dribbles and passes to D on a high post. (A) continues on and may get the ball back from D. Player B faked in and then "V'd" back and cut up court. Note path of E. If this procedure fails, an alternate method is necessary (see next diagram).

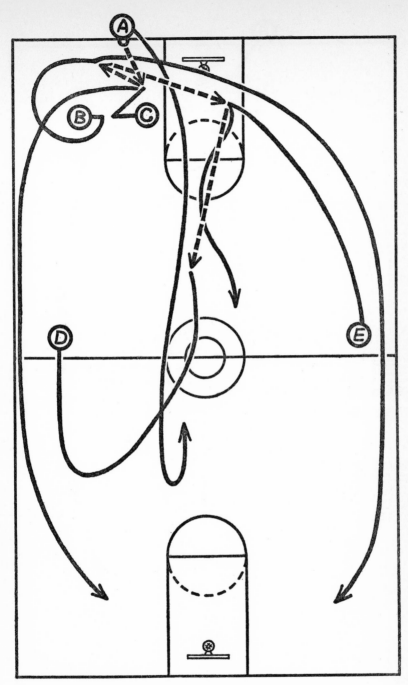

DIAGRAM 81. *Variation #1, Coming out of the Man-to-man Press.* (A)
passed to C but did not get the ball back. He continues on up court as
shown. When B sees that A does not get the ball he swings around as
shown and receives the pass from C. E, on the other side of the court, also
saw that A did not get the ball and continued his move to the position
shown and received the ball from B. E now passes the ball to D on the
high post and follows his pass up court. (D has several options: dribble
or pass to E, to A, or to B.)

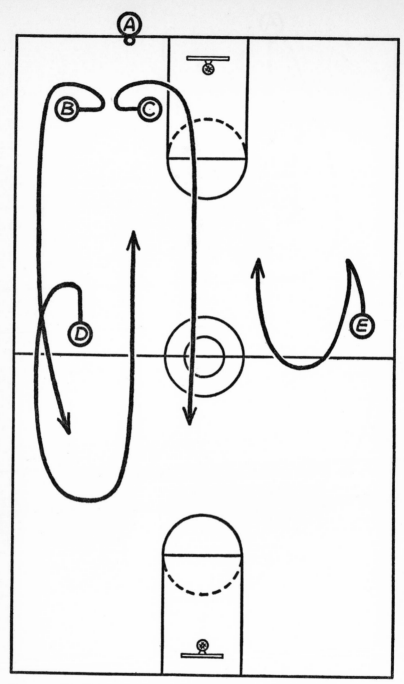

DIAGRAM 82. *Fishhook Variation, Coming out of the Man-to-man Press.*
(A) now tries to hit D and E in that order following their fishhooks. This
variation stresses the long cut and the long pass and is designed to keep
the opponents "honest."

DIAGRAM 83. *Trap Variation, Coming out of the Zone Press.* (A) passes
to B who delays an instant. A then runs behind chasers 1 and 2. At the
same time, B starts a dribble into the obvious trap (the clamp by opponents 1 and 2). Just before opponents 1 and 2 reach B he bounce-passes
to A. Now, with the basket hanger (E), A, C, and D have a "four on three"
situation on defense opponents 3, 4 and 5.

125

DIAGRAM 84. *Sideline Fishhook Variation, Coming out of the Zone Press.*
Player A passes to B. B delays a split second, apparently to give A time to
run behind defensive players X-1 and X-2. B now dribbles once and then
passes to C who has started up court, reversed and comes in fast for the
pass. E is ready to break down court to help out should C need his assistance.

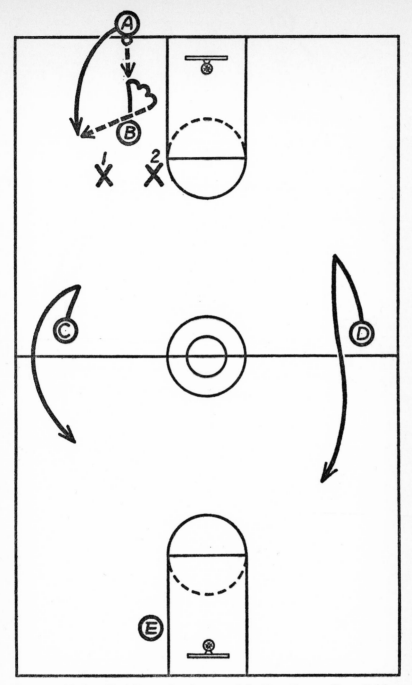

DIAGRAM 85. *Fast Trap Press, Coming out of the Zone Press.* Here, B fakes
going into clamp and hits A with the ball before he starts to go behind
defensive players X-1 and X-2. Teammates C and D go for the basket.
(Player B takes only one dribble before passing to A.)

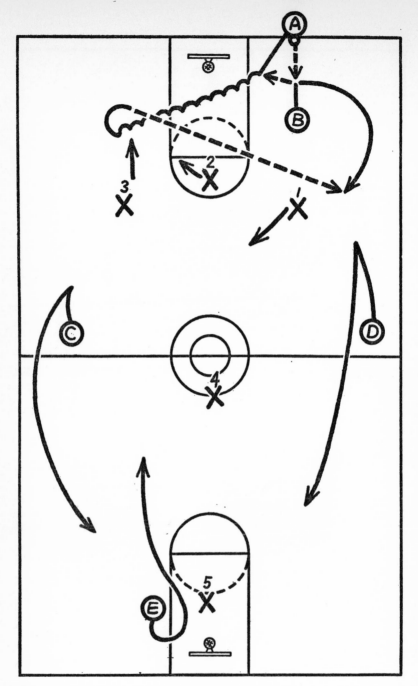

DIAGRAM 86. *Coming out of the Three-One-One Zone Press.* Player A hits B and receives the ball back. (A) immediately tries to drive to the outside of defensive opponent X-3. Opponents X-2 and X-3 will now try to put on the clamp. X-1 will probably drop back to put on the second clamp. For the offense, B, who has given the ball back to A, goes to the opposite side line. After A has drawn the defense over, he turns quickly away from the opponents and passes to B. Teammates C and D break as before. If defensive X-1 recovers or intercepts, A is at fault since the pass was not forced. B may dribble down or pass ahead to C, D, or E.

128

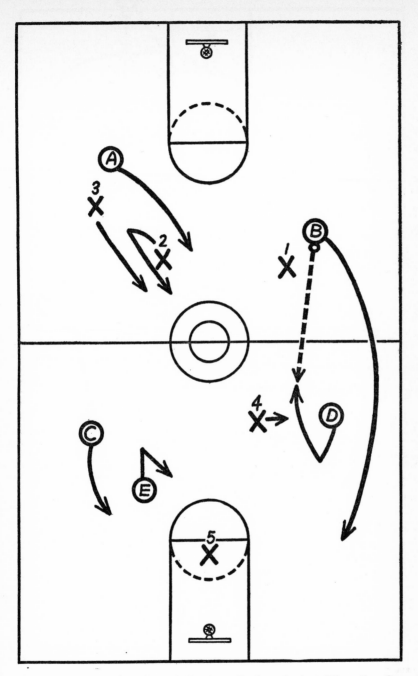

DIAGRAM 87. *Continuation of Previous Option Against Three-One-One Zone Press.* (A) passed across court to B who immediately hit teammate D and then cut up along the sideline. Player D is now ahead of the zone chasers and may pass down court to B, back to A, across court to C, ahead to E, or may dribble across the ten-second line and then hit a teammate before defense player X-4 reaches him.

MEETING CHINESE DEFENSES

In meeting Chinese defenses, we use the One-Three-One offense. By Chinese defenses, we mean combinations of zone with man-to-man, a one-man chaser with a box zone, two-man chasers with a triangle underneath, etc. Instead of figuring out what defense is being used, we go into our One-Three-One formation as soon as we meet a Chinese defense since we feel it will work against any type defense.

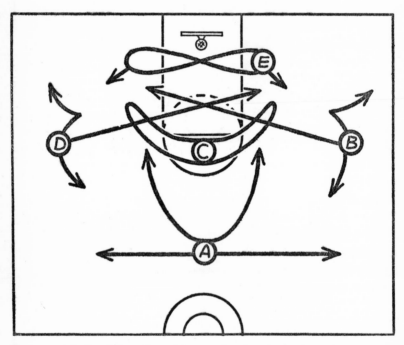

DIAGRAM 88. *One-Three-One Offense.* In the above One-Three-One attack, player A is the quarterback and is expected to set up the plays and take care of the defensive balance with the assistance of B and D. Should A drive in order to tighten up the defense, B or D must cover the back court. As in our attack against the various zone defenses, we set up triangles, drives, passes, and fill the open spots. Patience, good passing, plus poise and purposeful moves are the key to success in meeting the Chinese defenses.

9

Play Principles,
Feeding the Pivot
and Breakdown Drills

I do not believe in shackling my team with count-
less plays. They are given, at the most, four or five plays, and
most of these plays are based on beating one or two men and
not beating five men. Neither do I believe in spending the
whole night trying to feed the pivot. You can waste much time
and still not get results. Regarding break-down drills, there is
no play in basketball that cannot be done well with three men.
I think that all break-down drills should have a direct bearing
on your offense. For example, when I am using a break-down
drill to feed the pivot, I use three on the offense and three on
the defense working on nothing but feeding the pivot—a guard,
forward and center. We go into every type of maneuver such
as inside screening, outside screening, clearouts and swinging
the pivot. When we work on these plays, we work on them
alone.

The only time we use five-on-five for a break-down drill is
when we are using the Three-Out and Two-In offensive system.
This is because of the give-and-go, screening with and away
from the middle. Oftentimes in our lay-up practice we will use
a give-and-go drill or a screen drill.

In planning the attack principles the player's abilities must
be taken into consideration. The player is it! The style of play

will be successful or unsuccessful depending solely upon his ability to use the play under fire. If he lacks the necessary skills it is useless to attempt that style of play.

Many players possess special abilities which may be used in any system. Others are limited. If you have a big man who can score near the basket it would be silly to use him in the back court. A player with an excellent set shot should be used in his favorite shooting spot. The cutter and driver belongs in the back court where he can use give-and-go tactics. The hard-driving dribbler should also be used in the back court. So, too, should the smaller men who are fast and who possess feinting and maneuvering abilities.

After determining the abilities of the various players they should be placed in the attacking formations where their abilities can be utilized to the utmost. If the coach is caught with players who do not possess shooting, passing, or dribbling skills, then he has a real teaching job on his hands and must devote his time and practices to fundamentals.

All the Dartmouth practice drills have a direct bearing on our offensive and defensive game play.

Where possible the players may be divided into groups. This permits the coach to keep everyone busy. Further, placing them in groups enables the coach to combine good players with poor and the more expert can help coach the weaker players.

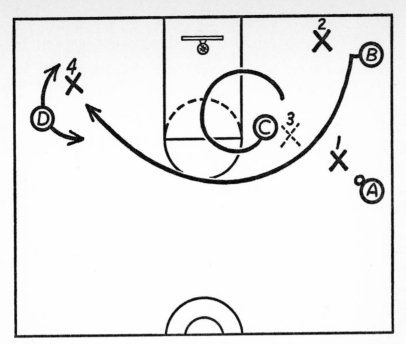

DIAGRAM 89. *Securing Pivot Position.* Because of player B's screen in front of the pivot position, pivot man C should be able to get a good position on the lane.

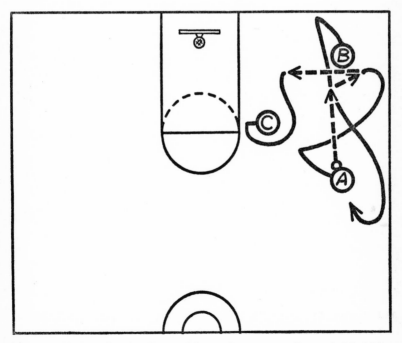

DIAGRAM 90. *Securing Feeding Position.* (A) passes to B, cuts behind him, and gets a return pass. B comes out to replace A's starting position. A now passes to the pivot man.

DIAGRAM 91. *Feeding the Pivot.* This drill is designed to develop the ability to feed the pivot with the defensive opponent playing in front, on the side, and in back of the "big" man.

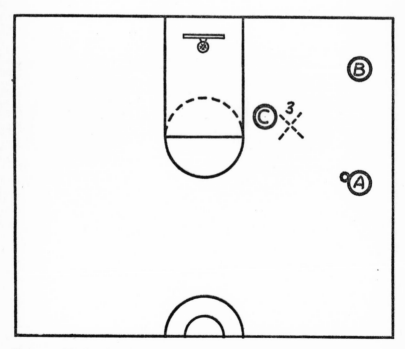

DIAGRAM 92. *Feeding the Pivot* (Continued). With a defensive man playing in front of the pivot player, we practice this move. Pivot man C starts for the opposite corner and then comes back as shown in the next diagram.

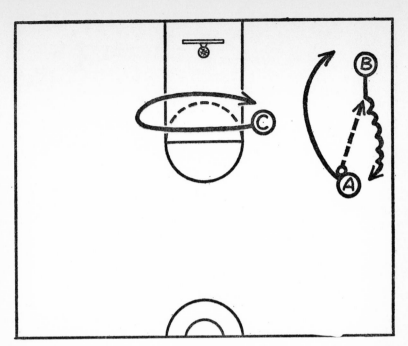

DIAGRAM 93. *Feeding the Pivot* (Continued). While the pivot man C is maneuvering for position, teammates A and B pass the ball and exchange positions.

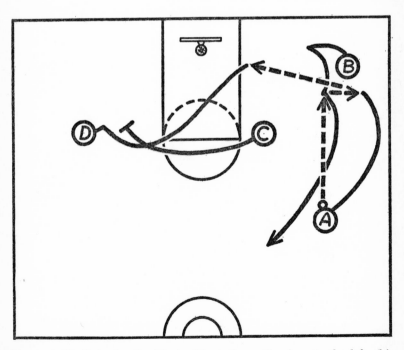

DIAGRAM 94. *Swinging the Pivot.* Pivot player C swings to the left (his right) so that D may replace him on the line. Teammates A and B pass the ball and exchange positions until they can feed player D who has now become the pivot man.

DIAGRAM 95. *Splitting the Pivot.* After A passes to C, he cuts as shown. B, who filled A's position in the back court, now cuts toward the basket and receives the ball from C.

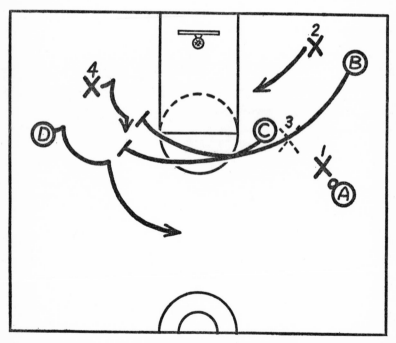

DIAGRAM 96. *Securing a One-on-One Situation.* Player C clears with teammate B, giving the impression that a double screen for player D is the objective. Player D fakes a cut and then makes his "V" and player A has a one-on-one situation. Good execution of the previous maneuvers will help this play.

DIAGRAM 97. *Setting up the Two-on-Two.* (A) passes to B, makes a back screen, and continues along the baseline to clear out for a two-on-two situation for B and C.

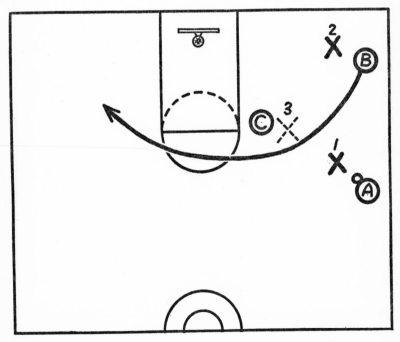

DIAGRAM 98. *Setting up a Two-on-Two* (Continued). Cornerman B clears across in front of the pivot player C without the ball. This now provides a two-on-two situation between A and C.

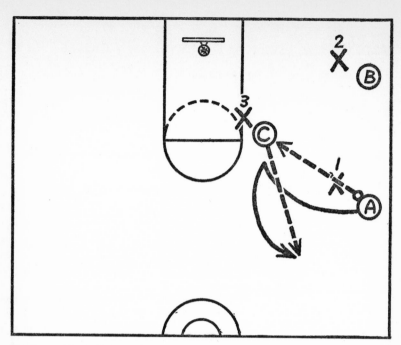

DIAGRAM 99. *Pull-Out Play for Shot.* When the defensive opponent is playing behind pivot player C, A feeds the pivot, cuts forward and then pulls right back. C passes the ball to A who takes the shot. Good follow-in is necessary here.

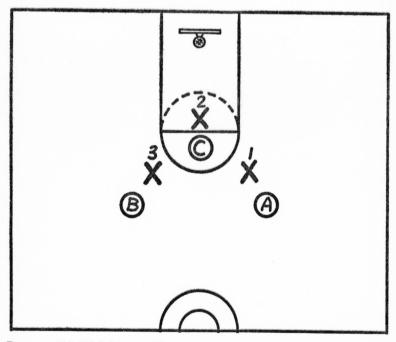

DIAGRAM 100. *High Pivot Drill.* In practicing our breakdown drill for the high pivot, we more or less employ free-lance cutting and passing. We exchange the ball until the high post can be hit and then we double cut as shown in the following diagram.

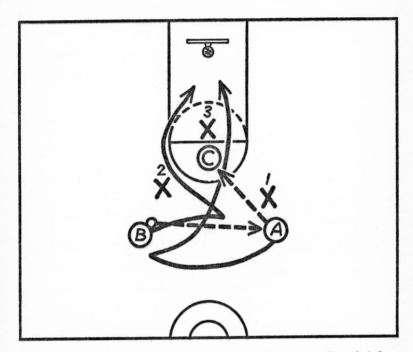

DIAGRAM 101. *The "V" and the High Pivot.* Teammates B and A have passed until they could hit the high post and then have used the "V" to cut past the post player C.

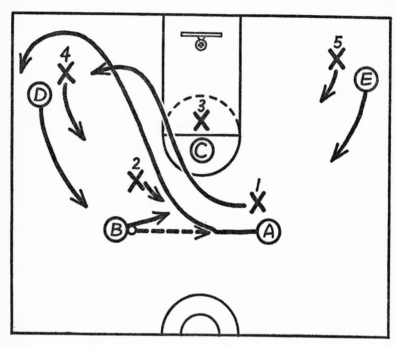

DIAGRAM 102. *The Weave and High Pivot.* The principle shown in the previous diagram is also incorporated into the five-man weave. Here, players A, B, D, and E, are executing the weave while the high post player (C) is waiting for the pass. C can secure some excellent practice by cutting to the base line and then coming out high for the pass.

DIAGRAM 103. *Splitting the Post.* (A) dribbles left, passes to C and reverses his cut. B fakes right and drives behind A's screen.

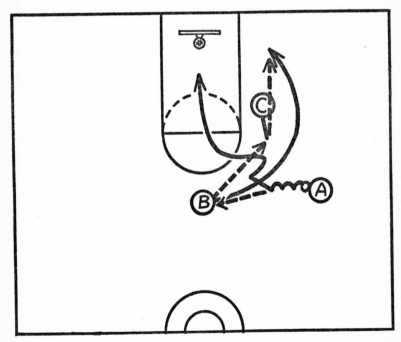

DIAGRAM 104. *Splitting the Post* (Continued). (A) dribbles left, passes to B and maneuvers as shown. B passes to C and cuts behind A's screen.

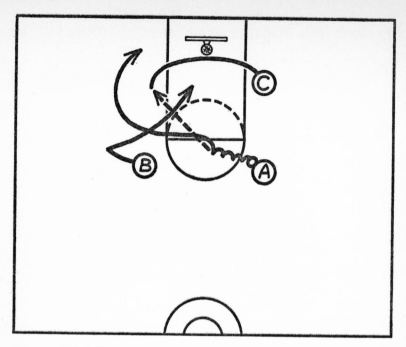

DIAGRAM 105. *Splitting the Post* (Continued). (A) dribbles to the left and feeds the pivot C. B trails A and then reverses his cut as shown. C feeds the player who breaks loose.

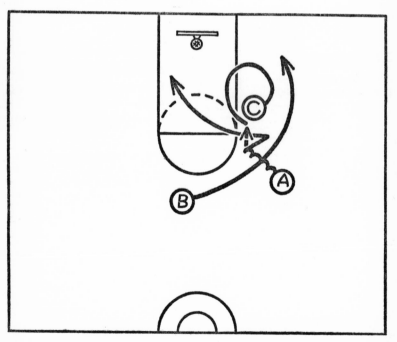

DIAGRAM 106. *Splitting the Post* (Continued). (A) dribbles left, feeds C, and maneuvers as shown. B drives to the right.

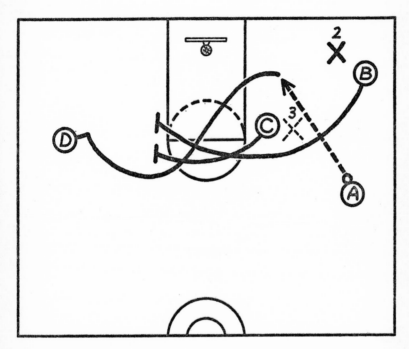

DIAGRAM 107. *Double Screen*. As player B gets one step past the pivot man (C), he is followed by C to set up a double-screen for D. This is a fine maneuver when the defensive man is playing in front of the pivot, because if defensive players X-2 and X-3 switch, C can come back and D can stay out of the play.

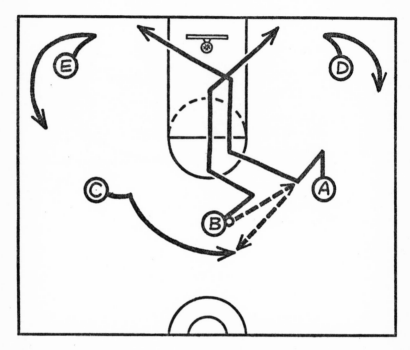

DIAGRAM 108. *Breakdown Drill for the Three-Two Offense.* This weave should be developed by starting without defensive opposition. As soon as it can be handled efficiently, defensive players can be used. Player B passes to A and cuts right. He then "V's" away and drives down the middle as we do in the give-and-go. When the cutter (B) reaches the lane, he cuts toward the base line and then on to the corner. (A) passes to C and cuts to the free-throw line before swinging off to the left corner. The pass and cut continues with each player raising his inside hand as he cuts, as is done in the give-and-go when expecting a return pass. The above drill can be used for give-and-go practice by lengthening the cut so that the cutting player drives clear "under" the basket before fanning out for the corner.

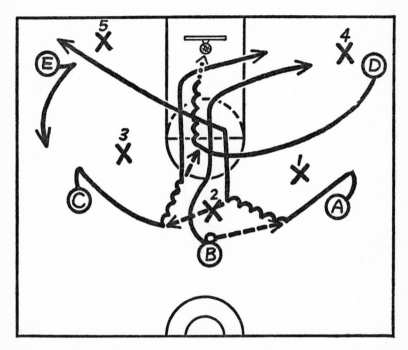

DIAGRAM 109. *Breakdown Drill* (Continued). When we add defensive men in this drill, we teach our boys what we call the "pass up." After we have been weaving and cutting down the middle for several exchanges, we start looking for the pass up. Here, instead of the man with the ball passing to the next receiver (as in the basic weave), he keeps the ball and drives. Each player must be taught to watch for the hole (daylight between himself and the basket), and drive for the basket with a "keeper" (dribbling-in instead of passing). In this diagram, player D has the opportunity to keep the ball instead of passing to E (providing he can see daylight).

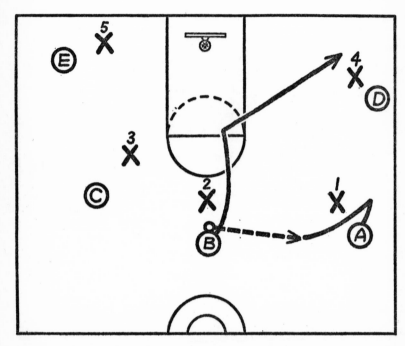

DIAGRAM 110. *Cutting Path.*   In the weave, the players should be taught to
go on either side of the defensive player so the middle cannot be clogged.
Here, player B passes to A and cuts on the same side as the pass.

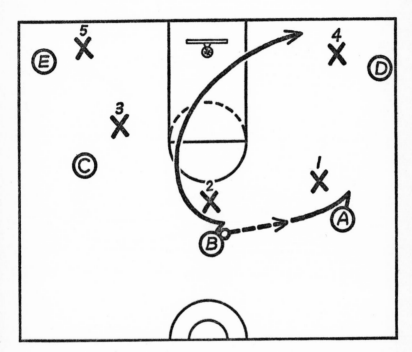

DIAGRAM 111. *Cutting Path* (Continued).   Here, player B passes to A and cuts on the side away from his teammate. Irrespective of the side taken in the cut down the middle, the player must observe continuity and cut to the proper corner.

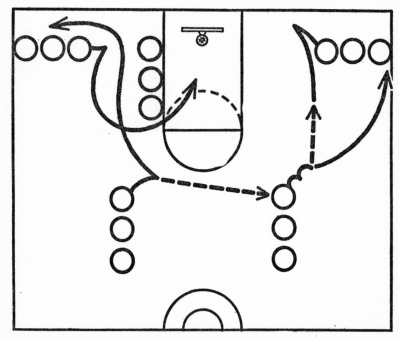

DIAGRAM 112. *Formation-Plays Drill.*   Several teams are selected and lined up in the formation to be practiced. The first team runs a play and, when it is completed, the players return to their respective positions at the end of each line.

10

Dartmouth's
Man-to-Man Defense

In today's basketball too much stress is being placed on offense and too little on defense. Now, when the word *defense* is mentioned to a boy, he looks at you in a sort of bewildered manner and seems to be wondering what the word means.

All coaches have experienced games when the ball just would not go in the basket for their players. On those nights, defense becomes vitally important and if you can stop the other team from scoring too readily while you are "cold" you can stay in the ball game—at least until you start hitting or the other team cools off.

I well remember how our Holy Cross team was fortunate enough to win the N.C.A.A. in 1947. In preparing for the tournament we stressed a lot of defense and hoped our team would not get the "Garden Jitters." Luckily, we did not. At any rate, defense was our biggest asset because not one of the teams we played (Navy, C.C.N.Y., Oklahoma) scored more than fifty points against us. I fully realize that scoring today is higher, but, relatively speaking, the results are the same.

A team which plays a strong defensive game need not worry about its offense. If it can meet an opponent's attack with confidence and determination and apply sound defensive principles, the offense will take care of itself.

Every high school or college coach loves to have at least one good defensive player who can "saddle" the opposition's high scoring ace. What a help that can be! I contend that any boy can do a creditable job if he puts his mind to it and works at it. And I further contend that in playing good team-defense you can still score in the high figures.

I had a boy at Muhlenberg by the name of Jim Capehart, a handsome, fast, lean and strong boy, almost 6′ 3″. Here was a real defensive player and he could really put the saddle on a good scorer. Yet he did everything wrong, turned his head, crossed his feet and watched his opponent's eyes. But they couldn't score on him! What did I do? I let him alone! Once in a while you'll get a boy like that who can't execute the fundamentals but still gets the job done. And right here I would like to say that it is not always necessary to match men with size, speed, etc.

Incidentally, one of the finest defensive men I ever coached in college was Gene Booth of Dartmouth. Booth was quick with his hands and always had good position. Two of his best feats were to hold both Forte of Columbia and Hundley of West Virginia to twelve points while they were averaging 28 points per game against other opponents.

Take a look at professional basketball today. What a great defensive player Bill Russell of the Boston Celtics is! Not only around the basket blocking shots and rebounding, but watch him guard a man! Bill Sharman, also of these same Celtics, is an excellent defensive player and still a high scorer. Slater Martin of the St. Louis Hawks is another fine defensive player. There are many others in the professional ranks.

The starting point in teaching defense is with a philosophy of defense which the players can recognize. If the coach is to do a good job of defensive coaching he must sell defense to the players and develop a feeling of individual and team pride in every player on the squad. Giving credit to the players is important. The more fuss you make about good blocking and rebounding and good individual and team guarding, the easier the task.

No boy should be taught the zone defense until he has mastered the man-to-man defense. It is much easier to learn zone defense after you know man-to-man, rather than the other way around. Bob Cousy, who had played practically nothing but zone defense in high school, can vouch for that. We worked him so much on man-to-man defense when he first came to Holy Cross that he nearly got discouraged.

The "in-line" position (between the opponent and the basket) is fundamentally sound. Yet there are many exceptions. For example, when opposing a player who always dribbles to the right when he has the ball, it is good defensive play to overshift to the left.

Defensive players should always try to move into a defensive position where they can see their assigned opponent as well as their teammate's opponents. If the defensive player can watch the ball without turning his head away from his opponent, he should do so. However, he should not try for an interception unless success is almost sure. If his opponent is a considerable distance away from the ball, the defensive player may sag or float to eliminate turning the head.

When the opponents rely upon a strong pivot attack, it is important that all defensive players try to help the teammate who has been assigned to stop the pivot man. By playing the man with the ball close, to discourage passes to the pivot, and by overshifting, sagging and floating, passes may be discouraged. Naturally, the man guarding the pivot scorer will try to play between his opponent and the ball.

Boxing-out and rebounding is often considered an individual responsibility. And, in certain instances, it can be so regarded. When a coach is fortunate in having an unusually tall re- bounder, he may be so proficient in controlling the defensive backboard that help is unnecessary. In such cases, many coaches pin the big boy with the responsibility of securing the ball and stress a quick outlet pass and a devastating fast break. However, most coaches will agree that boxing-out and rebound- ing is a team responsibility. If you can get your players to recognize its importance you have made a good start. Once they realize that the game is won "on the boards" they will work together at blocking-out and getting the ball.

The importance of team offensive and defensive balance is

recognized by every coach. In game after game we coaches see players become so engrossed in scoring that they forget to keep defensive balance. I am a strong believer in three-man offensive plays. The other two men should take care of the defensive balance.

In setting up an offense, the circulation plan should take care of defensive balance by forcing at least two players to move back to the defense. Many of the defensive team's fast break opportunities come about because the attacking players forget to "go through" with their circulation responsibilities. By using the whistle in the scrimmages and practice games to draw attention to defensive balance omissions and circulation errors, the coach can impress his players with the importance of these key defensive measures.

Stop the fast break: The fast break can change the complexion of a game in the twinkling of an eye. In game after game two teams will play evenly and appear to be well matched. Then, suddenly, one of the teams will find a flaw in the opponents' defensive balance and will score several quick baskets and then go on to an easy victory. Every player on the team should hustle back when the opponents start a fast break. How often have we seen one or two defensive players do a tremendous job of stopping a three-on-two situation only to have a "trailer" drive through and make a score after a shot or two has missed. If their teammates had hustled back the trailer would have been checked and the opponents would not have had two or three shots. Hustle pays off!

The following step-by-step moves are necessary in stopping the fast break:

1. Offensive and defensive balance must be maintained through circulation.
2. Good shots only should be attempted.
3. A good follow-in is important. The rebounder must be opposed as soon as he gets the ball, to prevent a good outlet pass.
4. The path of the outlet pass must be blocked and the ball intercepted if possible.

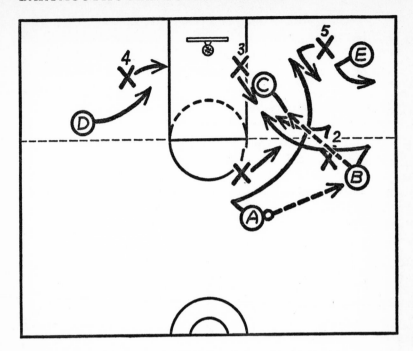

DIAGRAM 113. *Poor Defensive Balance*. The right word here is, "Terrible!" Besides being bad offensive basketball (crowded right side of the court), defensive balance is entirely missing. The above illustration may seem to be greatly exaggerated but it occurs all too often. In teaching defensive balance and poor offensive circulation, the coach should watch for circumstances like the above and immediately blow his whistle and point out the weaknesses.

Offensive players D and E are not concerned with the play and should be setting up the defensive balance by moving out to the back court. Here, a fumble by C, an interception by a defensive player or a deep rebound would undoubtedly result in an easy score by the opponents. The broken line extending from the side lines and through the free-throw line shows that the offensive team will have no one back nor in a position to set up defensive balance.

5. The usual receivers of the outlet pass should be covered to discourage the first pass.

6. First man back directs traffic and covers the dangerous under basket lay-up area. He should work back slowly until he reaches the lane. During this retreat he should feint to come out to the man with the ball or a potential

receiver until he reaches a point four or five feet from the
basket.

7. The dribbler must be stopped. This is the responsibility
   of second man back who tries to force the dribbler to
   either side of the court. If possible, the dribbler should be
   checked or stopped near the center of the court.

8. If the dribbler cannot be stopped and the first man back is
   double-teamed, the second man must assist in setting up
   the "shuttle."

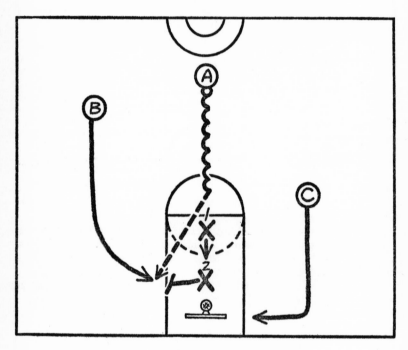

(Diagram 114-A)

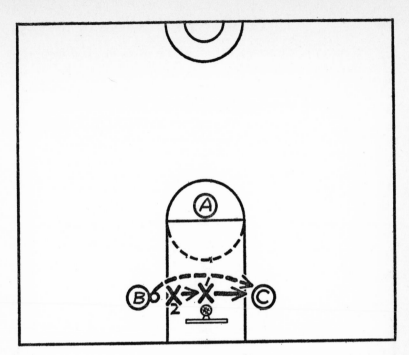

(Diagram 114–B)

(Diagram 114–C)

155

(Diagram 114–D)

DIAGRAM 114. *The Shuttle.* In drawing A, defensive players X-1 and X-2 are outnumbered by opponents A, B, and C. On a signal, defensive player X-1 moves out to the line to oppose A while teammate X-2 moves back under the basket. When A passes the ball to B, defensive player X-2 moves out to cover him and defensive teammate X-1 drops back under the basket. In drawing B, the ball has been passed from player B across to C. Defensive player X-1 now covers C and his defensive teammate X-2 moves under the basket. In drawing C, the ball is passed from attacking player C back to A. Defensive player X-2 now moves out to guard A, and defensive teammate X-1 covers the under-basket area. In drawing D, we have the original starting position of the shuttle but the defensive players have exchanged places due to the movement of the ball.

DARTMOUTH'S MAN-TO-MAN DEFENSE

A good defensive player always has good position on his man and good balance. Whether you take the boxer's stance with one foot back of the other or the baseball infielder's stance with feet even, be sure you have both position and balance. Keep your hands up at all times, not at the same level necessarily, but one high and one low or in a position which is advantageous to you.

Next, be sure to never cross your feet. Use the shuffle, lifting one foot and shuffling the other. Never leave your feet on a fake shot for that is when your opponent will go by you. Do not turn your head, for that is the cue for your opponent to give-and-go. And one thing we stress is to watch the "belt buckle" of your opponent—not his eyes or his feet! Where his belly button goes—he must go! Find out whether your opponent is slow or fast. Is he shifty? Does he cut left and right or does he go only one way? Find out his favorite shots and tricks and how he plays under the basket. Stay between your man and the basket!

If he is in mid-court or even in the corner without the ball— give him room! Watch him out of the corner of one eye (without turning the head) and the play with the other. In this way you may intercept a pass or pick up a loose man. If you lose your man, run under the basket since that is where you will most likely find him. The closer your man moves to the basket, the tighter you play him. If he does not have the ball, try and keep him from getting it.

Now, here is what we advise for the defensive position. Stay low and be ready to move in any direction by shuffling your feet. Keep your head up and your knees bent. Your weight should be slightly forward but not too much. Keep your hands up at all times. We have a little saying here at Dartmouth: "Don't play defense like the hands of a clock when they read six o'clock, but like the hands of a clock when they read ten minutes to six."

In switching, try to drive your opponent toward the side. Don't let him make the turn on you—flatten him out!

DEFENSING THE BIG MAN

The chief attack of many strong teams is built around a big man who can score or handle the ball efficiently for cutting teammates. Good man-to-man defense means that the defensive player must move around and about the pivot player in an effort to screen him away from the ball. When the pivot player maneuvers in trying to secure a good shooting position, it may be wise to block his path, double-team him or zone his scoring area.

DIAGRAM 115. *Forcing Opponent to the Side.* Here, defensive X-3 has stepped forward on the switch and has forced A toward the sidelines.

DIAGRAM 116. *Poor Switching.* Defensive player X-3 has fallen back and has permitted attacking player A to drive toward the basket.

Now for defensive pivot play. First of all, in playing defense against a pivot man you must try to stop him from getting the ball. That is most important. If a pivot man is playing close to the basket, the defensive player should play in front of him. Naturally, the defensive man should keep to the side of the ball, never letting the opponent get more than one arm's length away from him. If the opponent tries the "dummy" play, the defensive player can always get help from a corner man. After all, the opponent cannot use the dummy play all night (it does need perfect execution).

If the pivot man is playing medium (half way up the free-throw lane), the defensive player can guard his opponent three ways. First, in front; three quarters; or again, half-way. The three-quarter defense means that a defensive player plays partly in front and partly on the side of the opponent, keeping his arm in front of the pivot player to keep his teammates from passing the ball in to him. The defensive player should try to keep the opponent from getting position by moving with him, sometimes in back of him, around to the other side, even going in front of him occasionally to get to the other side.

The defensive player must keep a hand up to knock away a pass. In guarding in the "half-way" position, the defensive player stands on a line between the ball and the basket at the *side* of the pivot man. And, as in the other positions, the defensive player keeps his arms up, especially on the ball side. He should move around him, back of him, and in front, but he should be sure he is never worse than halfway.

Once the pivot man gets the ball, the defensive man must not play the big man tight and allow him to roll in on him. He should loosen up and keep his hands up. If the big man is going to shoot, he should be forced to do it going away. It is impossible to stop all the big man's shots, but the defensive player must, in this case, take the lesser of two evils.

When a pivot man plays high (in the outer-half of the free-throw circle or the same distance from the basket but on the side), the defensive player should play in back of him (about one arm's length). When this is done it is impossible to try to keep him from getting the ball. Here, the defensive player must maintain the proper position so that the big opponent cannot go in on him. And, the defensive player should also be sure to leave space so his teammates can slide through directly behind the pivot man if they cannot fight through in front. Again, the hands must be up and the defensive player must constantly talk to his teammates who are in danger of getting run into the post. By saying: "Head up!" or: "Be careful!" the teammates will be warned. If a teammate is picked off, the defensive man must call the switch. The play is in front of him all the time and there is no excuse for his *not* making the call.

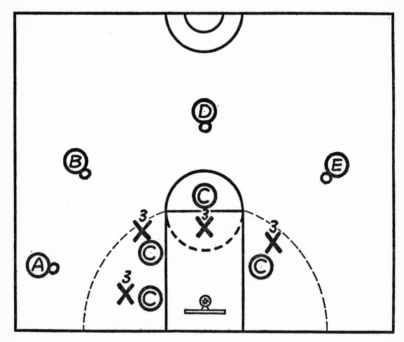

DIAGRAM 117. *Guarding the Pivot Man.* Defensive player X-3 is shown in the various guarding positions recommended in opposing the pivot man. The broken line represents the fifteen (15) foot area. When the pivot man plays inside this area, defensive player X-3 moves to the "in-front" position when possible.

Defensing the big man often becomes a "team" job. Not all of us are lucky enough to get an outstanding big man year after year who can stop the opponents' pivot players. Fortunate indeed is the coach who has a good big man who is an expert defensive player and can handle the giants. I feel like a million when a big man shows up—good, bad or indifferent. So, when we meet a team with an outstanding pivot player who is too good for our big man, defensing becomes a team problem.

Team defensing of the big man presumes that the opponent with the ball who is in a "feeding" position will be played closely, aggressively, and that every effort will be made to prevent him from passing the ball to the pivot player. Teammates who are in position to do so will be expected to sag and float as well as double-team the pivot player.

When other methods fail to stop the big man it may be wise to attempt some sort of a zone which will prevent him from getting the ball. Clair Bee's One-Three-One zone was designed expressly for this purpose and may be the solution. Naturally, the Two-Three zone defense throttles much of the big man's effectiveness close to the basket, but it permits good outside shooting opportunities. (See Chapter 11.)

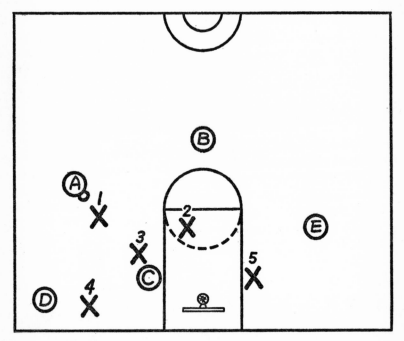

DIAGRAM 118. *Team Defensing the Big Man.* With the ball in offensive player A's possession, defensive player X-1 is playing him aggressively. Since the offensive pivot man is within the 15-foot circle, defensive player X-3 is playing in front of C. Defensive teammate X-5 has floated away from opponent E and is ready to try for an interception should a shot or float pass be thrown over teammate X-3's head. If C should get the ball, X-3 and X-5 will double-team him. Defensive players X-2 and X-4 have dropped away from their opponents to help out. Both anticipate a pass to their respective opponents (B and D), and are ready to cover them.

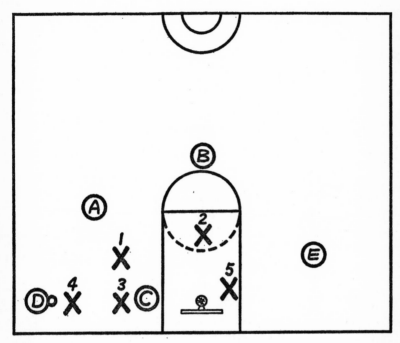

DIAGRAM 119. *Team Defensing the Big Man* (Continued). The ball has been passed from opponent A to D. Now, defensive player X-4 covers D closely. Teammate X-3 moves with the pivot player (C) and maintains his in-front position. Defensive teammates X-1, X-2, and X-5, have sagged and floated until the formation resembles a One-Two-Two zone formation. Naturally, D may throw the ball back to A or to B or E but defensive players X-1, X-2, and X-5 anticipate such passes and are ready to quickly cover their respective opponents.

11

Dartmouth's Zone Defenses

M an-to-man is considered the basic defense at Dartmouth. For that reason we do not devote too much time to the perfection of our zones. However, we feel that adding one or two zones to our defense catalog is necessary for several reasons.

One: We may encounter a team which is proficient in the use of a screen and pivot attack but is not equipped with good outside shooters. If we feel the screen and pivot attack will give us trouble, we will use either the Two-One-Two or the One-Two-Two zone.

Two: We feel that in teaching our players to use the zone defense we are also teaching them how to best attack the zone.

Three: We may wish to use the zone as a change of pace or to throw our opponents off balance.

Four: When we are being scouted excessively we may use the zone in several games against weaker opponents so that the scouts will carry back information which will not be detrimental to our basic defense (man-to-man).

Five: Against some opponents the use of a zone press may prove effective, and the teaching of a set zone will make our zone press more easy to learn.

Six: We often find two or three players on our squad who are expert in the use of the zone because of high school training or natural skills, and it is to our advantage to capitalize on their special abilities.

The zone is popular in high school and it seems that more and more college coaches are turning to this type of defense. This means that experience in the use of the zone and in developing effective means to attack the zone are important team assets.

The zone is strong in setting up good team rebounding positions and in getting off a fast break. Further, it is effective in checking a strong screening attack and will give good protection to big men who are slow or who make too many fouls when playing man-to-man defense.

The zone is weak against a good shooting team. It is also weak against a team which breaks hard and often. This is chiefly due to the fact that the big men who generally operate in the front line of a team's attack are at a disadvantage in getting back to their defensive under-basket area in time to get into their zone positions. It would seem logical that the application of the zone on a large court would be a disadvantage. However, we have all seen the zone used successfully on a full sized court so that point would seem to be debatable.

The Two-One-Two zone is, in my opinion, the best all-around zone in use because it provides fairly good protection under the basket. We like the One-Two-Two zone because the slides are simple and, again, in my opinion, the man with the ball can be covered more quickly than in any other zone. We use these two zones to the exclusion of any others. Again, it is our opinion that proficiency in one or two zones is far more advantageous than trying to master four or five different types.

In our use of the zone, we make adjustments from game to game. Our zone defenses are always aggressive after the ball and not merely a sliding affair with a half-hearted attempt at extension of the arms and sluggish use of the feet. We make sure it will be difficult for our opponents to pass to one another by immediately attacking the man with the ball. This play of the ball is similar to a press and we seek to double-team if possible.

Our use of the zone makes it imperative that our players

work. In fact, our players feel that the zone we use is much more tiring than the man-to-man defense.

When the opponents send a man through, we do not bother with him. However, we make sure he does not get a return pass. To make sure he will not get this return pass we will go with him a step or two to discourage or intercept a give-and-go type of play. If a return pass is not forthcoming, we let the cutter go on through the zone.

All through our use of the zone we try to impress upon our players that we are playing the ball. The man in possession of the ball is the key target and the man guarding him must attack aggressively. The other players are concerned chiefly with getting into position, anticipating the next pass, and, above all, staying alert to the better than fifty per cent possibility of an interception.

Keep in mind that the fast break is quick to get into action from any type of zone. At Dartmouth, we advise our players that forty per cent of the effectiveness of the zone is reflected in the burden of a fast break possibility, which is placed upon the attacking opponents. If they do not keep a strong defensive balance, we must concentrate upon getting away fast to outnumber them. If they keep two or three men back they are handicapped in effectively attacking our zone. It is not unusual for one or two of our chasers to break when the opponents take a shot. Naturally, the chasers who break must feel that the ball is rebounding into the hands of one of our own players or that the opponents are not in good follow-in positions.

The Dartmouth Two-One-Two Zone: This zone is a compromise between the Three-Two and the Two-Three zones. We like it because it gives us strength in the middle and under the basket. We like two strong "chasers" with the desire to hustle and the leg power to back up the desire. The middle man is the key man. He takes care of the opponents' pivot man and must be a fast thinker and a good rebounder. The two back men must be fast enough to cover the corners and be good rebounders.

DIAGRAM 120. *Zone Moves.* (Based on movement of ball): The movement of men is of little concern other than to prevent the return pass. However, we prefer to cover the opponents' men so they can't drive against us.

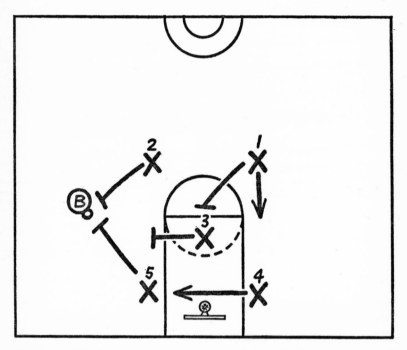

DIAGRAM 121. *Zone Moves* (Continued). When the ball is at "B" defensive player X-5 comes out to cover. Defensive X-4 fills X-5's spot. Sometimes X-4 will go halfway between the lane and the side line depending on where the opponent's base-line man is playing. Defensive X-3 plays the offensive's pivot man near the free-throw line or assists X-5 in a double-team play. Defensive player X-1 will cover the weak side on a man-to-man basis. If there is no opponent on the weak side, he will drop back in front of the free-throw line. We are still aggressive.

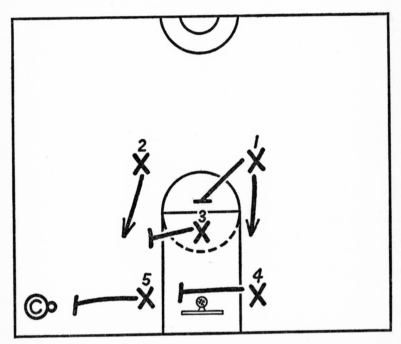

DIAGRAM 122. *Zone Moves* (Continued). When the ball is in the corner "C", defensive X-5 covers. Defensive X-4 moves over nearly to the middle of the lane, and defensive X-3 plays anyone in the pivot position man-to-man. If there is no opponent in the pivot position, X-3 will drop back slightly in front of the basket. Defensive X-2 takes a position between the free-throw line and the side line.

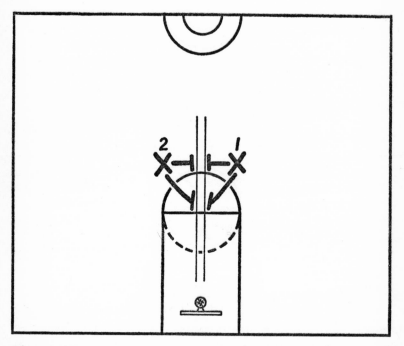

DIAGRAM 123. *Territory Limitations.* Defensive players X-1 and X-2 never cross this imaginary line. This is to prevent the long slide which would give opponents on the respective "chaser's" side of the court the time for a good shot.

DIAGRAM 124. *High Post Defense.* When the ball is in possession of an opponent in the high post position "C", defensive player X-3 plays him on a man-to-man basis. Defensive chasers X-1 and X-2 tighten and drop back. Defensive X-4 and X-5 close in toward the three-second lane.

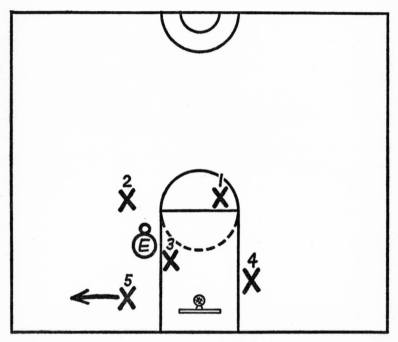

DIAGRAM 125. *Inside Pivot Defense.* When an opponent has the ball beside the lane "E", defensive player X-3 plays him on a man-to-man basis. Defensive X-5 will move toward the left corner prepared to cover, and defensive 4 will retain his position near the right side of the lane. Defensive players X-1 and X-2 drop back as shown.

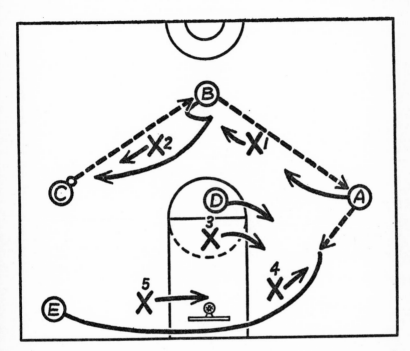

DIAGRAM 126. *Two-One-Two Zone Moves.* When C, above, passes to B and cuts toward the basket, we make sure he does not get a return pass before we let him go. He becomes defensive player X-4's responsibility. (See the next diagram.)

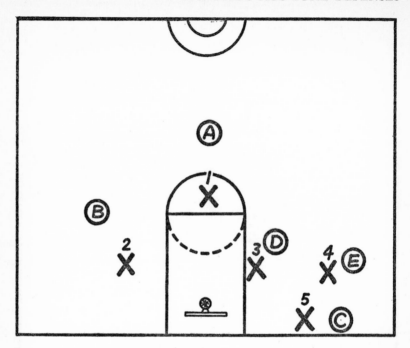

DIAGRAM 127. *Zone Moves* (Continued).   After A receives the pass from B, he passes to E and moves to the center of the attacking formation. B replaced C. Defensive X-1 holds his position, defensive player X-3 moves with D; defensive X-4 has left C and picked up E who received the ball from A. Defensive X-5 has shifted over to cover C. Defensive player X-2 has moved counter clock-wise to protect the weak side.

THE DARTMOUTH ONE-TWO-TWO ZONE

Our moves in this defense are simple and regular and are governed entirely by the movement of the ball and the man with it. Naturally, in the use of both defenses, we employ the same tactics on each side of the court. Ball position and the shooting range of the opponents determine how close we go to the man with the ball.

Shot charts taken on our opponents for at least two or three games have considerable influence in determining the shifting of our men to meet the pertinent situation. We never let any player drive or start to drive.

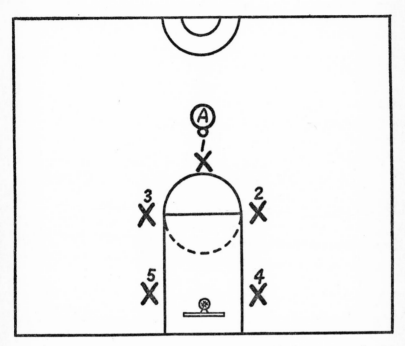

DIAGRAM 128. *One Two-Two Zone Positions.* This is our normal position with the ball in the position shown ("A").

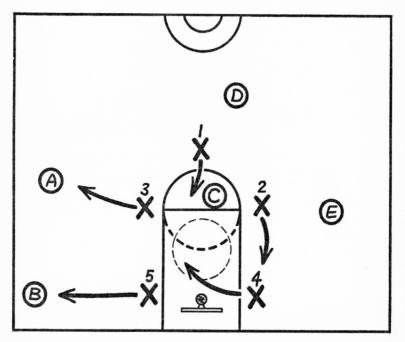

DIAGRAM 129. *One-Two-Two Zone Moves.* With the ball in the possession of A as shown, defensive X-3 moves out to cover. And, with the ball at
A, defensive X-5 comes over to cover opponent B. Teammate defensive
X-4 covers the area shown by the lines of the broken circle and defensive
X-2 drops back to fill X-4's spot on the right side of the lane. Defensive
chaser X-1 drops back in the outer half of the free-throw circle at the side
of the ball.

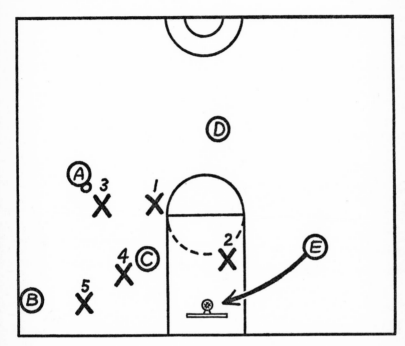

DIAGRAM 130. *Zone Moves* (Continued). Attacking player C has moved to a position beside the lane and is covered by defensive X-4. Note defensive player X-2. He must now watch C as well as E because of teammate X-4's defensive position.

DIAGRAM 131. *Zone Moves* (Continued). (A) passed the ball to B and defensive player X-5 covered him. Defensive X-4 dropped away from C to cover E and defensive X-2 moved closer to the basket. Defensive player X-1 has moved back to help teammate X-2.

ZONE THE BIG MAN

Reference was made in Chapter 10 to the use of a zone in defensing the big man. At Dartmouth we have used Clair Bee's One-Three-One zone as well as the Two-Three in attempting to stop the exceptionally tall player.

DIAGRAM 132. The One-Three-One zone may utilize straight slides or use the revolving principle to keep three men between the ball and the basket (also to set up a double-team situation on the pivot man anywhere in the 15-foot area). In the diagram above, the ball is at A and defensive player X-1 opposes him aggressively. If the ball is passed over the head of X-1 to the man on the high post (C), X-1 is expected to fall back and help X-2 double-team C. If the ball is passed to B, X-5 will play him aggressively and teammates X-2 and X-3 will maintain the three-men-in-line principle. X-1 and X-4 will drop back to the position shown in the following diagram.

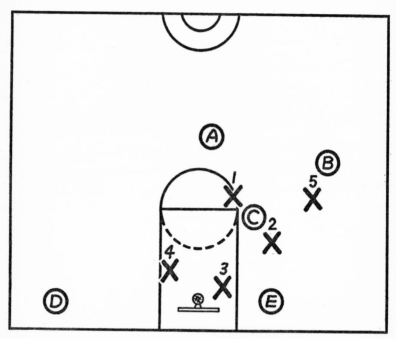

DIAGRAM 133. *One-Three-One Zone* (Continued). The ball was passed from offensive player A to teammate B. Defensive player X-5 now plays B aggressively and is backed up in the three-in-line principle by teammates X-2 and X-3. The pivot player (C) is practically surrounded. It is assumed that offensive player E will move to the right corner. See the following diagram to check the moves made to cover the corner.

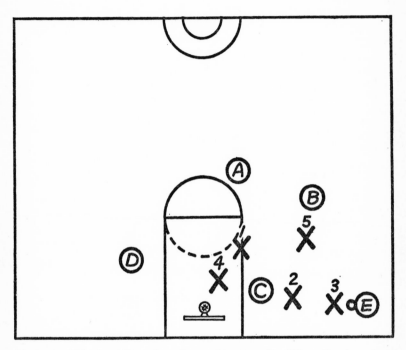

DIAGRAM 134. *One-Three-One Zone* (Continued). The offensive player E cut to the corner and his teammate (B) passed the ball to him. Defensive player X-3 immediately covered E since the offensive pivot man was moving down the lane behind teammate X-2. By the time the ball reached E in the corner the formation resembled a One-Two-Two zone formation. Defensive player X-3 now covers the ball aggressively, X-2 is in the middle and the third man of the three-men-in-line position is taken by X-4. The offensive big man is again practically surrounded.

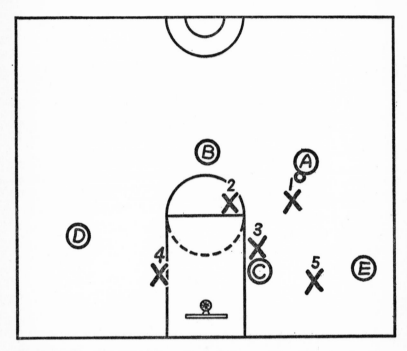

DIAGRAM 135. *The Two-Three Zone Defense.* The slides in the Two-Three zone defense are fairly simple and it can be seen in the above example that the big man (C) is fairly well defensed. Naturally, side and down-the-middle shots will be available but it must be kept in mind that the chief concern in this particular situation is the opponent's big man and his defense.

12

Defense Auxiliary and Drills

The man-to-man defense is subject to a number of variations. Most of these have developed because of zone influences such as floating, playing the ball for interceptions, and massing in front of the basket. Other types utilize man-to-man and zone principles and advance to meet the attack all over the court.

THE PRESS

If it is late in the game and you are behind in the score, it is wise to gamble and disregard assigned men. Here, opposing the nearest opponent, talking, pointing and hustling are imperative. Players should try not to foul. The objective is to hurry the opponents and to try to force them to make bad passes and give your team the opportunity to make an interception.

Some teams run wild in this situation, chasing the ball haphazardly, leaving a man wide open when an interception opportunity is not present, trying to double-team an opponent when the possibility is slim, and all too often make the disastrous mistake of leaving an opponent unguarded under the basket.

When applying the man-to-man (even the zone press in certain situations) it is often impossible to find an open man. The pressing player caught in this situation should retreat to his own backcourt to protect against a long cut and an easy basket. However, he must do more than retreat. He must try to locate the loose player, point him out, and help out by picking up the closest opponent so that a teammate can pick up the loose man.

The press is valueless unless all players work as a team in applying it. How often you have observed three or four players apply a perfect press only to see one or two teammates loafing. Here a splendid opportunity may have been overlooked and thrown away just because a couple of "lazy" players did not hustle.

Most coaches like to place the ball in the hands of their best dribbler when they are opposed by a press. The dribbler must be stopped. Frequently, he will turn his back to avoid an opponent and this offers a splendid opportunity to double-team. It is important that the dribbler be slowed down in your offensive half of the court if possible. Once he crosses the ten-second line he will be in position to feed a loose man and the opponents may score easily.

In opposing players when the ball is out-of-bounds in the opponents' back court, or deep in their back court, the pressing players should play inside, close to their opponents, and be ready for a break in any direction. It is good strategy to play in front of a player when he is in his front court and the ball is in his back court. Here, however, the player guarding near the opponents' basket must be ready to pick up a "loose" man and call out for help if necessary.

Right here, a little story might be apropos to the press. We were playing Colby on a Christmas trip and we planned to use a zone press against them. When the teams lined up, Johnny Jones called out: "Merry Christmas, Colby. Here comes the zone press!"

DARTMOUTH'S PRESSING DEFENSES

At Dartmouth, we believe in making any press an aggressive one. Since it is mostly a desperation defense—we gamble. Or, if we are trying to force the opponents into mistakes in order to upset them, we may try it at any time during any game. No matter when used, we are aggressive in covering the ball; double-teaming, switching, and in making attempts to secure the ball.

The man-to-man press has been most effective for general use but we use two types of the zone press from time to time.

In the man-to-man press, we harass the man out of bounds with the ball, play the in-court men closely and on the inside.

In the zone press, we set up in a Two-Two-One or in a One-Two-One-One. Both zone presses are based on territory assignments with optional privileges, which permit the men to help out in teammates' zones and attempt double-teaming and interceptions.

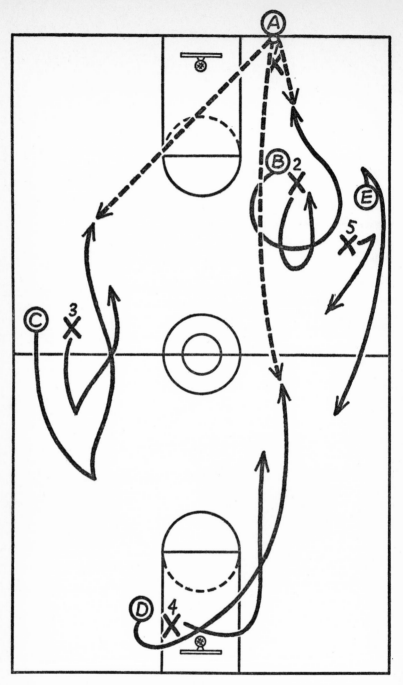

DIAGRAM 136. *Man-to-Man Press Positions.* We will leave our immediate opponent at any time to double-team another opponent. We will switch on every cross and play on the inside when the opponents play near the sidelines (try to force them to the center of the court).

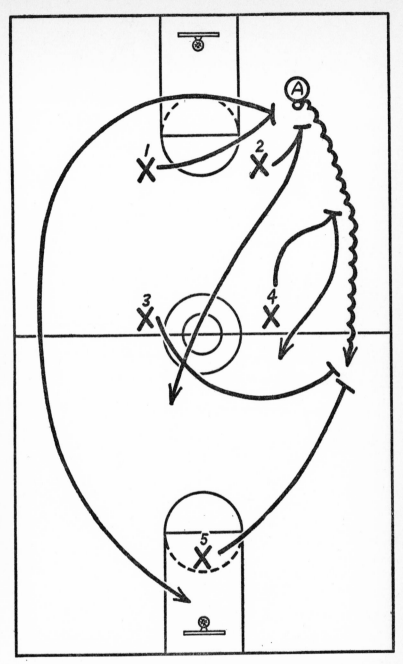

DIAGRAM 137. *Two-Two-One Press Moves.* (A) has the ball and defensive players X-1 and X-2 are trying to clamp him. Defensive player X-4 is backing them up to stop A should he escape from teammates X-1 and X-2. The second clamp is put on by defensive players X-3 and X-5. (Note that player X-1 covers the under-basket area when X-5 advances. On the opposite side of the court, defensive X-2 would cover.)

DIAGRAM 138. *One-Two-One-One Zone Press Moves.* Pressing player X-2 has moved to his left to cover opponent B. Teammate X-1 follows quickly and tries to join X-2 in developing a double-team situation. Teammates X-3, X-4, and X-5 move across to the left side of the court, alert for an opportunity to intercept a pass or help out. Defensive player X-5 is responsible for the under-basket area and directing the defensive set-up once the opponents cross the 10-second line.

COMBINATION DEFENSES

Combinations have an advantage over straight defenses since they can be varied to meet the abilities of the players on hand more readily than the man-to-man or zone defenses. These "Chinese" defenses originated with the development of the five-man defense. And, as the zone and man-to-man defenses became known and utilized, certain coaches began to experiment in shifting, switching, floating, and combining man-to-man and zone defense principles.

At Dartmouth, it is felt that our regular man-to-man defense, our two zone defenses and some use of sagging, floating and pressing principles are all we can efficiently apply.

DEFENSE DRILLS

Defense drills are so important that they should be used from the first day of practice to the last. On first thought, they would seem to be necessary only in the early season practices. However, the pre-season period is too short to develop thoroughly the defensive habits which will be used in every game. Review of the defensive (and offensive) drills are absolutely necessary throughout the season. In addition to individual defensive drills, team defensive drills are important in teaching player cohesion.

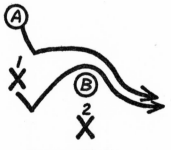

(Diagram 139–A)

(Diagram 139–B)

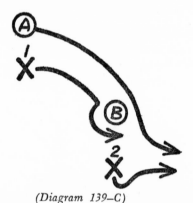

(Diagram 139–C)

DIAGRAM 139. *Front, Slide, Switch.* In drawing A, defensive player X-1 has been maneuvered back by his opponent. However, when attacking player A cuts, he leaves room for defensive X-1 to go in "front" of the post player (B).

In drawing B, defensive player X-1 has been forced too far back toward his basket. Now, when his opponent (A) cuts close to the post man (B), defensive player 1 must "slide" between opponent B and his teammate (X-2). (Defensive player X-2 should move about two arms length back to allow X-1 room to slide through.)

In drawing C, attacking player A has again maneuvered defensive player X-1 back. This time, however, attacking player A has a better cutting angle and defensive player X-1 must either "slide" or "switch." In this particular situation, defensive player X-2 has called "Switch!" and has moved to cover attacking player A. Defensive player X-1 must now "switch" to cover opponent B.

DIAGRAM 140. *One-on-One and One-on-Two Defensive Drill.* On the left side of the court, defensive player X-1 is opposing A on a one-on-one basis. If A is able to score, or secure the rebound following a shot, he keeps the ball and defensive X-1 must remain on the defense. If defensive player X-1 steals the ball or secures the rebound, he becomes the offensive player.

On the right side of the court we have a one-on-two situation. Offensive player B, only is allowed to shoot. His offensive teammate (C) screens and passes to him and B tries to break free from defensive player X-2 for a shot.

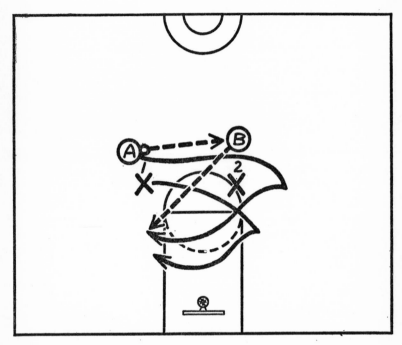

DIAGRAM 141. *Two-on-Two Defensive Drill.* Offensive players A and B pass, cut, dribble and use moving and set screens in breaking free for a score. Defensive players X-1 and X-2 must front, slide and switch in guarding A and B. Under no circumstances are they to go behind (see following diagram).

DIAGRAM 142. *Two-on-Two Defensive Drill* (Continued). Defensive player X-1 has permitted his opponent (A) to maneuver him into a "back" defensive position instead of going front or using the slide (moving between B and his teammate X-2).

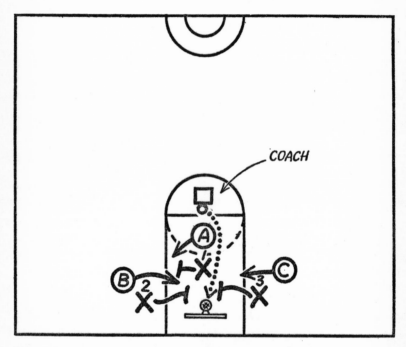

DIAGRAM 143. *Three-Man Blocking-Out Drill.* Attacking players A, B and
C are facing the basket as are defensive players X-1, X-2 and X-3. The
coach shoots (a lid can be placed over the basket) and the defensive players (X-1, X-2 and X-3) block A, B and C away from the rebound. The objective is to block-out the attacking players so effectively that the ball will
fall untouched to the floor.

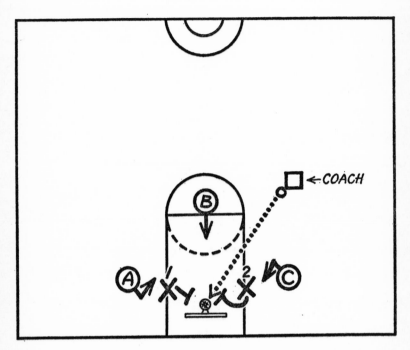

DIAGRAM 144. *Two-Man Blocking-Out Drill.* Defensive players X-1 and X-2 are outnumbered by A, B and C in this blocking-out drill. Defensive players X-1 and X-2 must block out their three opponents until the ball hits the floor.

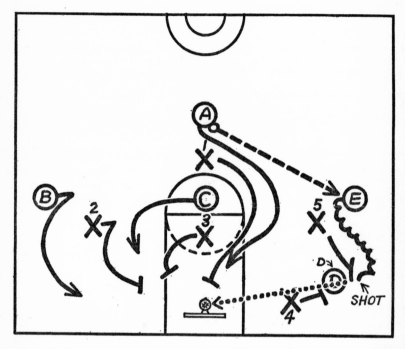

DIAGRAM 145. *Team Blocking-Out Drill.* The attacking players (A, B, C, D and E) pass and cut and move the ball until they can get off a shot. As soon as the attacking player shoots, the coach blasts his whistle and all players stop as quickly as possible. The coach then checks the blocking-out positions of the defensive players.

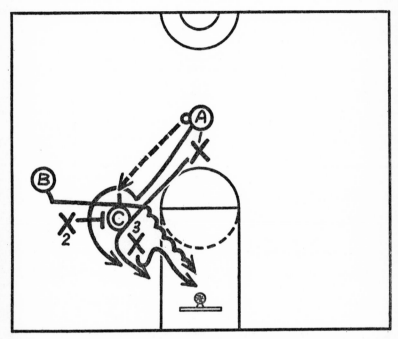

DIAGRAM 146. *Switch on Ball Drill.* This drill is designed to develop the switching ability of the defensive player (X-3). Attacking player A passes to C and cuts as shown. Defensive player X-3 backs up as C cuts past to allow teammate X-1 to slide through. However, he calls "switch!" and picks up the second cutter (B) when the ball is passed to him. Defensive player X-2 switches to cover C.

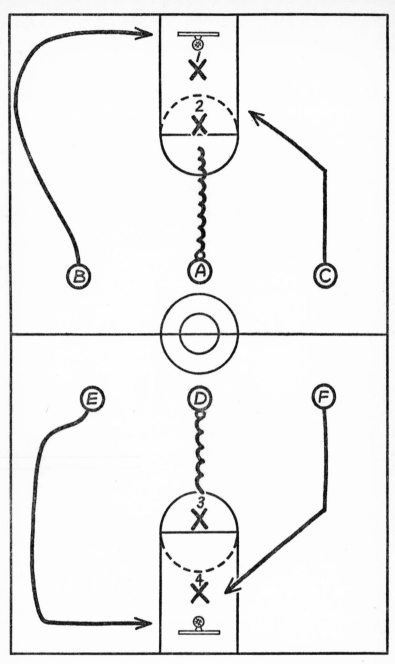

DIAGRAM 147. *Defensive Shuttle Drill.* Three attacking players here attempt to score against two defensive players. Both ends of the court are used and the defensive players *must* use the defensive shuttle to break up the scoring attempts.

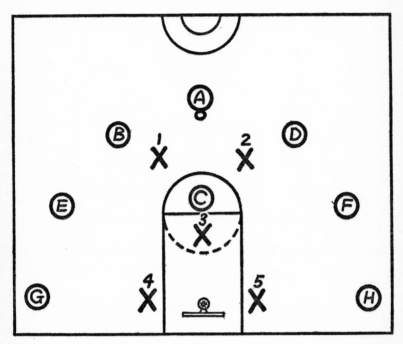

DIAGRAM 148. *Two-One-Two Zone Drill.* Eight attacking players oppose the zone set up by defensive players X-1, X-2, X-3, X-4 and X-5. The purpose of the drill is to teach the correct zone shifts and slides. (The ball is passed slowly at first and then the passes are speeded up to force fast shifting by the zone players.)

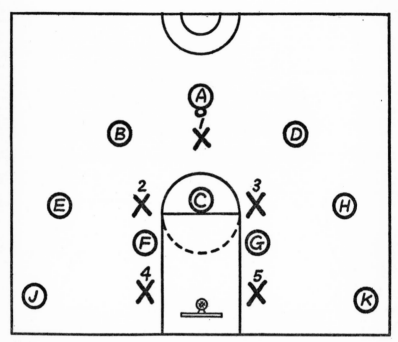

DIAGRAM 149. *One-Two-Two Zone Drill.* As in the Two-One-Two zone drill, the defensive players are outnumbered. Here, ten opponents are attacking the five zone players. (Pivot players have been added.)

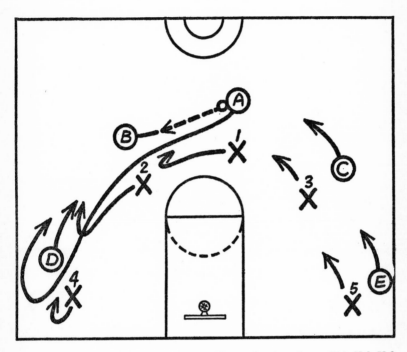

DIAGRAM 150. *Screen-Switch Defense Drill.* Defensive players X-1, X-2, X-3, X-4 and X-5 switch on every cross. This drill calls for fast footwork by the defensive players. (No shots permitted.)

13

Practice Program

Ivy League Regulations prohibit more than one pre-season organization meeting and we hold it about a week before our first practice. All players bring their note books to this meeting and are instructed which notes to take down.

We generally talk about the season ahead and what is expected with respect to training and studies. The game and practice sessions schedule has been mimeographed and we pass out the copies at the end of the meeting. The players are told the number of men we carry on our traveling squad and the number who will dress at home.

We advise the players to dispel all fear of making mistakes, emphasizing hustle, teamwork and morale. Regardless of the caliber of our opposition we always feel we can win. At this time we also advise them that they can't enjoy some of the things the other students do—in other words, they must sacrifice a little, but they will be better for it later on in school and in life.

The players are told that if they have any gripes they should take them up with the head coach so that they can be talked through. Coaches make mistakes as well as players. We are all human. Let's have fun playing but let's always play to win. We have certain things to do . . . Let's do them! If a player is not willing to put out, we do not want him to come out for the team.

All positions are open. We tell the candidates that they should not get discouraged at the beginning of practice if the coaches do not seem to be paying much attention to them. That will come later on. At no time are the players to wear their feelings on their sleeves. Color, creed, names—these bear no preference. . . .

A player's feet must be perfect for him to feel like playing his best. At the first sign of blisters the player must go to the trainer. He must be sure his shoes fit well. He should be prompt for practice and notify the coach if he can't be present or on time.

We discuss the manager's duties, equipment needed each day at practice, time to report, charts and forms used, and managers' duties in general. The managers are responsible for the condition and issue of basketballs, jumping ropes, different colored jerseys, the blackboard, and all playing and statistical charts. Since a trainer is always present at practice, medical supplies are his responsibility.

The managers are told never to discuss with the ball players their chances of making the team; to never discuss with the student body anything relative to the squad; and never to criticize the playing of an individual or to discuss any player in a derogatory manner with any person, during practice or at any other time, or to tell players ahead of time whether or not they are making the trips. The managers are responsible for the bulletin boards. Schedules, practices dates and times, scouting reports, trips and their itineraries are posted on these boards. The managers also serve as liaisons between the players and the coach. "Let's be a happy family!"

At this time, we make sure all sophomores are familiarized with our nomenclature. We diagram our man-to-man offense (the Pivot and the Three Out-Two In) and the plays for each formation, as well as our basic attack to oppose the various zone defenses.

Our basic man-to-man defense is also covered at this time. We issue mimeographed copies of the 26 Magic Numbers for study purposes, as well as our training rules.

When we start basketball practice, I do not want my boys in top shape for the first game. Let's say, almost in shape, so that they must play themselves into shape. Then, in three, four, or five games they are fit. Like most coaches, our practices are longer at the beginning of the season than they are later on. We begin with a two or two-and-a-half hour practice session and by late season we are down to about an hour with usually the day off after a game. "If you eat too much ice cream, you get sick!"

We start each practice with rope jumping and then go into our various pre-season drills. I will not try to tell you what drills to use. There are hundreds of good ones. We use passing drills for about a week; shooting drills; fast breaks; one-on-one; one-on-two; two-on-two; skeleton switching drills; jump-ball drills, and rebound drills. The one-on-one, one-on-two, and fast break drills are practiced every day. We stagger the others so the boys do not get tired of them.

We start our team work with half-floor drills, trying to get our offenses smoothed out. But if the defense players get the ball either through an interception or rebound, they may break for the opposite basket. This means we are always practicing the fast break and the defense for it as well as defensive balance.

We work gradually into whole floor scrimmages and get to the point where we simulate game play a little every day. During this period we use the break down drills described in the previous chapters.

During our half-floor practices, we frequently designate a player from either team go to the free-throw line and attempt a free-throw or two to accustom him to shooting under game conditions. Naturally, our offensive and defensive formations, our continuities, and play movements are covered.

We have one rule with respect to our scrimmages in which you may be especially interested. If we have eight men who we feel must carry the brunt of our hopes during the season, we never play those eight men against one another. We'll start a scrimmage with the first five playing against the ninth, tenth, eleventh, twelfth, and thirteenth men on the squad.

We substitute our sixth, seventh and eighth men freely for the players we consider our first five. We want those eight men to learn to play together and not against one another. This makes for better morale and spirit. If any of the other players can move up, we move a man down.

We gradually work our zone offense and defense into the practices. Up to now, it has been all man-to-man. Then, we add the man-to-man press (both offense and defense) and the zone press (both ways). Finally we get to the point where we can cover any part of our offensive and defensive repertory during any practice session.

We spend a lot of time on jump balls, the position each player should take at the offensive and defensive baskets, and the formations to be used when the tap is "ours" or "theirs." Out-of-bounds plays go in last. But, during all this time, we will use any break-down drill we think we need.

I think levity has its place in athletics so we like to have a little fun on the floor. I'll often use one of my favorite sayings such as: "How much rice can a Chinaman eat?" "Scrambled eggs!" "French pastry!" "Bread and Butter!" "You look like the keystone cops!" etc. But I expect the boys to turn it off at the proper time.

Basketball practices should not be as distasteful as going to the dentist. A player will often apply one of my sayings to express his personal disgust with himself when he realizes he has made a mistake.

I always visit with my team in the dressing room after practice. I may talk to all of them informally or talk directly to an individual player. Maybe a particular boy has done well in practice but I neglected to give him a little credit out on the floor. If so, I'll say: "Tom, I thought you looked good today."

Perhaps another boy has been going badly in practice; he is real tense. I may call him aside and ask him if there is any trouble at home; about his parents; how he is feeling physically. Then, to relieve matters a little, I may ask whether or not he got a letter from his girl friend lately. It is surprising the answers I get. Some boys do not like to be corrected in front of others. In this case, I arrange to meet them in the office or take advantage of any other opportunity I may have to get them alone. I ignore some players and go after others. The players seem to respond to this procedure.

There are some players who feel slighted if you do not bawl them out—feeling, perhaps, that you do not think much of them as a player. When I sense this, I ask them about their studies; kid them a little; try to make them smile. I like to listen to the boys kid one another. At the end, I tell them I'll see them tomorrow and leave. However, I make sure to warn them when we have a tough game coming up.

If a boy has been injured during practice, I make sure to check up on him before leaving. At this time I talk to the trainer and check whether or not he should go to the infirmary. All kids appreciate the interest of the coach in their physical and mental well being. . . .

I do get tough when the need arises. Real tough! I think every squad must be dressed down a couple of times during the season. I do not care if the players are sullen as long as they are not mutinous. I don't think a coach can win a popularity contest with his squad and still do a good coaching job. An old pro once told me something I'll never forget. He said: "Doggie, you must coach with your head, not with your heart."

I think a happy medium can be maintained. I think a good player-coach relationship is vital to success. Coaches have great influence upon the boys they coach. I want my players to feel free and eager to come to me with their personal as well as their basketball problems. Maybe I can be of help. . . .

One of the first things I tell my squad at the beginning of practice is to dispel all fear of making a mistake. And I'll tell them I don't care how many mistakes a player makes if, when he makes them, he's trying 100 per cent. On the other hand, he can't keep doing wrong. I want competitors. "Worse than a quitter is the boy who won't try. . . ."

I love speed. You can't substitute for speed. If I have two boys who are almost equal in ability, I'll favor the boy with the speed even though the slower boy has more experience. A player with speed can make mistakes and often recover.

I prefer a team that has balanced scoring rather than a team which boasts of a high scorer who makes all the points. It makes it tougher for the opponents' defense when they have to concentrate on five opponents rather than one "star."

We work quite a bit on defense. I think defense still has a vital place in basketball. There are nights when your team is cold. A good defense comes in handy at that time. I know it's difficult to get a player in modern basketball to think of defense, but I believe in giving anyone playing a good defensive game a great deal of credit so the team will feel defense is as important as the offense. We try to keep our team defensive minded to a degree that will help us to win.

14

Practice Session Outlines

The daily practice outlines which follow will provide the coach and his players with fundamental drills for all phases of the game and equip the team with a number of offenses, situation formations and plays. The coach's offensive and defensive check lists have been completely covered. (See Chapter 17.)

The time spent on the various items will, naturally, vary with the desires of the coach and the progress of his players. However, at Dartmouth, the time schedules and the corresponding activities are substantially those observed from the first day of practice right up to the first game.

As previously stated, I prepare my practice outlines previous to each week's practice work. The outlines are, naturally, built around the game schedule so that our training requirements will not be left to chance. Certain team needs may change the program but essentially the outline is followed.

The following outlines are those we use at Dartmouth and show the material to be covered and the time which should be devoted to each drill. Every day a new drill or some new feature should be added to the practice program to keep interest high.

PRACTICE 1

3:00 P.M. *All players jump rope for five (5) minutes.*
3:05 P.M. *Free shooting. All players.* (Have as many balls on the floor as possible. We want our players to handle and shoot a ball like apple pie and ice cream.)

3:15 P.M. *Passing.* The squad is formed in two "facing" lines six (6) feet apart (a ball for each two players).

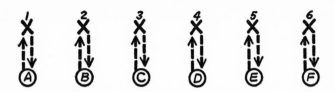

DIAGRAM 151. *Passing Drill Formation.* All passes are practiced and the players back up for the long throws. The coach quickly calls out the type of pass and demands snappy execution.

    Passes:
    1. Catcher's throw (right and left).
    2. Two-hand chest pass.
    3. Bounce passes. Right, left, one and two hands.
    4. Two-hand overhead.
    5. Dribble pass (for our weave).
    6. Roll (on floor).
    7. Hook pass. Right, left. (Fast break weapon).

3:20 P.M. *Shooting Practice:*
    1. Lay-ups left and right.
    2. Down the middle.

3:25 P.M. *Set Shots:*
    1. Players in pairs screen for one another.
    2. Cut in front and behind teammate for set shot.
    3 After passing ball and blocking off for teammate's set shot, turn around and wave hand in his face.
    4. Practice front give-and-go.

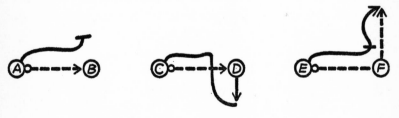

DIAGRAM 152. *Pairing-up for screens and shots.*

3:30 P.M. *Jump-shot drill:*

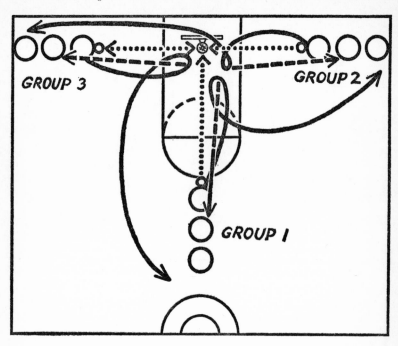

DIAGRAM 153. *Jump-shot Drill.* Three balls are in play. When a player from group 1 shoots, he gets the ball and passes it back to the same group. He now goes to group 2. Group 2 players move to group 3. Group 3 players to group 1. Players must make 22 for 50. To add an incentive the players count the consecutive shots made.

3:40 P.M. *Fast break practice.* Skeleton.

3:55 P.M. *One-on-One:*

    1. From right.

    2. From left.

    3. From middle.

    4. Both baskets.

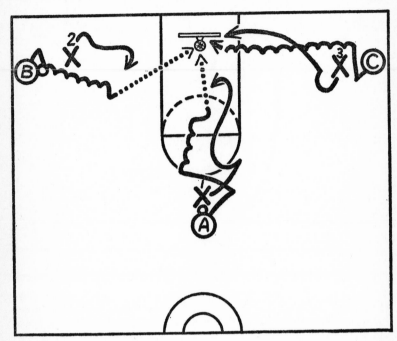

DIAGRAM 154. *One-on-One Drill.* This drill is good practice for offensive as well as defensive players.

4:00 P.M. *One-on-Two:*

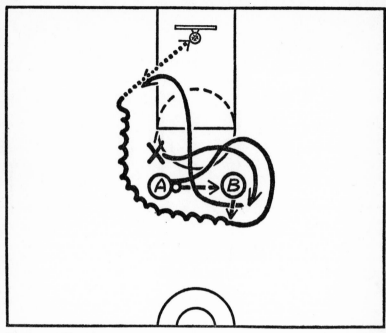

DIAGRAM 155. *One-on-Two Defensive Drill.*   Defensive X-1 is guarding offense player A. Only offense player A can shoot. Offense player B can do anything except shoot. When offense players A and B finish their turns they move to the defense. Offense players A and B must keep moving and passing until they manage a good screen or block so that offense player A can shoot.

4:05 P.M. *Switching practice:*

DIAGRAM 156. *Switching Drill Without Ball.* Players work in groups of four. The offense players make any move they wish in order to trick defensive players. The defensive players use only two words—"stay" and "switch"—to govern their moves.

4:10 P.M. *Jump ball practice:*

DIAGRAM 157. *Jump Ball Drill.* Players work in groups of three. One man tosses the ball—the other two jump. After the tap, they alternate positions.

4:15 P.M. *Blackboard talk:*
    1. Small blackboard on side of floor.
    2. Go over plays given at skull meeting.
    3. Make sure every player knows assignments.
4:20 P.M. *Practice of basic plays:*

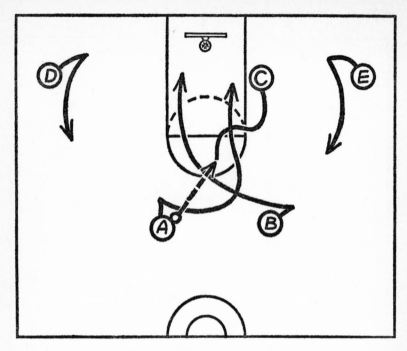

DIAGRAM 158. *Basic Plays Drill.*

Group 1 runs a play and is followed by second, third and other groups in turn. All run the same play. No defense.
1. Running screen. Right and left.
2. Flood play. Right and left.
3. Scissors play. Right and left.
4. Simple scissors.
5. Double screen.

4:35 P.M. *Running and passing:*

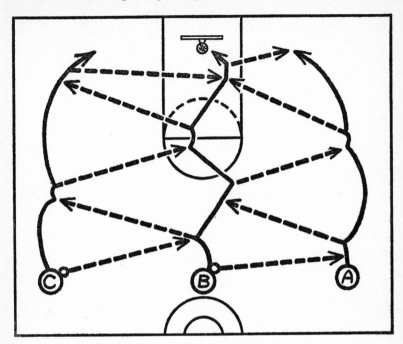

DIAGRAM 159. *Running and Passing Drill.* Players B and C each have a ball. Player B starts the drill by passing to teammate A. As soon as B passes, he looks for a pass from player C. He receives the ball from C and immediately returns the pass. Now, player B gets the ball from teammate A. He now passes the ball back to teammate A and receives a ball from teammate C. He returns the ball to teammate C and the drill continues. Players A, B, and C, run down the floor and back and the next group follows. (Coach should compliment the group which performs the drill the best.)

4:45 P.M. *Free-throw shooting:*

Each player must make eight (8) "one-and-one" shots out of ten (10) before he stops. The shooter reports how many times he tried before he was successful. Here is the way we do it:

In order for a player to get a bonus shot (free throw) on the "one and one" he must make the first free throw. If he makes the first and the second shot that counts as one. He must make eight of these.

If he misses the first shot he does not get the bonus shot so it counts as a miss. If the player makes the first shot and misses the bonus shot, that also counts as a miss. Naturally, if the player misses the three first shots or three second shots out of ten, he must start over. Each time a player starts over, it is considered another try.

Since this is the first day of practice it may be regarded as an orientation practice and the coach will probably not expect perfect performance. The coach can cut the practice short if he desires or extend the time so that the drills and other techniques may be better mastered. *We do not believe in running laps after practice.* While the free-throw shooting is going on, the other players practice their weaknesses—shooting, dribbling, passing, etc.

PRACTICE 2

3:00 P.M. *All players jump rope for five (5) minutes.*
3:05 P.M. *Free Shooting. All players.*
3:15 P.M. *Passing practice (two lines).*
3:20 P.M. *Lay-up shooting practice.*
3:25 P.M. *Set-shot practice.*
3:30 P.M. *Jump-shot practice (3 balls).*
3:40 P.M. *Fast break drill.*
3:55 P.M. *One-on-One.*
4:00 P.M. *One-on-Two.*
4:05 P.M. *Back-tracking practice:*

DIAGRAM 160. *Back Tracking Drill.* The players work in pairs—one of fense and one defense player. Six players run backward and six players run forward. The players run in straight lines down the floor and back with the offensive players running as fast as they can and with the defensive players (running backward) trying to stay in front of their matched "men" as long as possible. The players change offense and defense positions coming back up the court. Offense and defense players must run at full speed and must not slow down. When it appears that an offense player will run into his defense player, he runs around his man. The defense players try to stay in front of their opponent as long as possible but even after the offense player passes the defense player, the defense player must keep running backward at full speed. The players will improve rapidly as they repeat this practice.

4:10 P.M. *Reaction practice:*

DIAGRAM 161. *Reaction Drill.* The players form in a single line with one player in front of the line with a ball. This player passes the ball to the first man in the line who taps the ball back or to either side where the man behind him can catch it before it hits the floor. The players progress as shown below.

4:15 P.M. *Quick review of skeleton drill* (Plays 1, 2, 3, 4, and 5 from the regular pivot offense).

4:20 P.M. *Half-court pivot offense practice:*

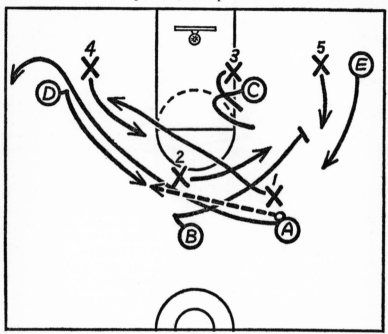

DIAGRAM 162. *Screen Practice Drill.* The attacking players keep running our weave and employ inside, outside, and back screens. Free lance play is permitted in this practice. However, any play is used when the situation permits. When the defense secures the ball the fast break is permitted. The offense players must try to stop the break. When the break is completed or checked, a blast of the whistle brings the players back for continued practice on the offense.

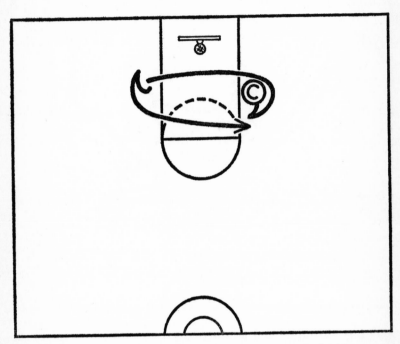

DIAGRAM 163. *Moving Pivot Drill.* This is used to teach the big man to keep moving in order to get position. The coach can move from one position to another and have the center work to get into position.

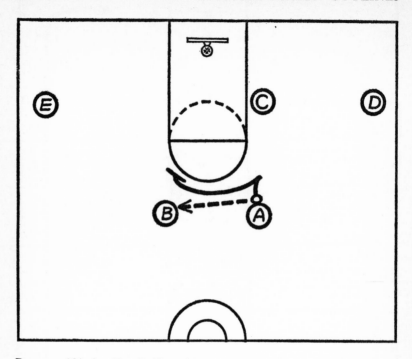

Diagram 164. *Set Shot Drill.* This is a drill we use to teach all men in the weave to set up screens for one another so they can get set shots.

4:55 p.m. *Running and passing drill* (two balls—three men).
5:00 p.m. *Free-throw shooting:* Eight (8) "one and one's."

PRACTICE 3

3:00 p.m. *All players jump rope for five (5) minutes.*
3:05 p.m. *Free shooting. All players.*
3:15 p.m. *Passing practice (two lines).*
3:20 p.m. *Lay-up shooting practice.*
3:25 p.m. *Set-shot practice.*
3:30 p.m. *Jump-shot practice (3 balls).*
3:40 p.m. *Fast break and shuttle practice:*

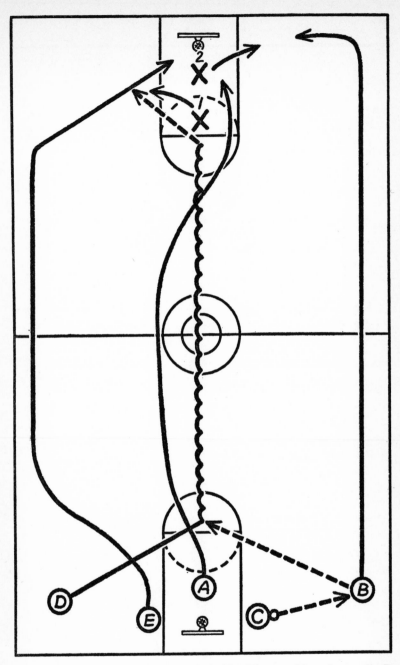

DIAGRAM 165. *Fast Break and Shuttle Drill.* The attacking players (A, B, C, D, and E) use our standard fast break to advance into scoring territory. Defensive players X-1 and X-2 employ the shuttle in an attempt to check a close shot.

3:55 P.M. *Switching practice drill without ball.*

4:00 P.M. *One-on-One.*

4:05 P.M. *One-on-Two.*

4:10 P.M. *Held ball practice.*

4:15 P.M. *Half-court practice (pivot offense versus man-to-man defense):* Free lance and plays. At frequent intervals call time and set up certain plays. The defense will still fast break when they get the ball and the offense players will try to stop the fast break. (Remember that we do not work our first eight or nine men against one another.) We use our first five (probable) with our sixth, seventh, eighth and ninth men substituting for them.

4:45 P.M. *Work plays against half-court defense players (any play.)*

4:55 P.M. *Passing and running drill (two balls—three men).*

5:00 P.M. *Free-throw shooting.*

15

Practice Sessions
Four Through Eight

PRACTICE 4

3:00 P.M. *All players jump rope for five (5) minutes.*

3:05 P.M. *Free shooting. All players.*

3:15 P.M. *Passing practice (two lines).*

3:20 P.M. *Lay-up shooting practice.*

3:25 P.M. *Set-shooting (two against two):*
In this drill, each twosome takes as many set shots as possible. The shooting players retrieve the ball after a shot and the retriever quickly passes the ball back to his partner who then shoots and does the same. The first pair to make ten successful shots wins. Winners play winners and losers play losers until there is a final champion. This lends competition and levity and the players get a kick out of it. This drill is used a lot by the "pros." (If there are not enough baskets, keep the players who are not shooting busy with drill work.)

3:35 P.M. *Jump-shot Practice:*

3:40 P.M. *Fast-break with two men on defense.*

3:55 P.M. *Back-track practice.*

4:00 P.M. *One-on One.*

4:05 P.M. *One-on-Two.*

4:10 P.M. *Two-on-Two:*
Here, we play two defense players against two offense

players stressing screening and switching. Players must use "stay" and "switch" when on the defense.

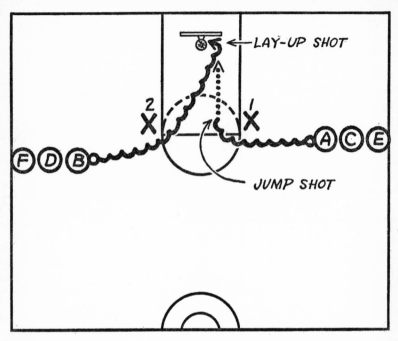

DIAGRAM 166. *Stop and Shoot Drill.* The coach and an assistant or manager stand on each side of the free-throw line, where it joins the lane. The players form lines on each side of the court and dribble alternately around the person standing at the free-throw line. If the coach calls: "Hip!" the player must immediately stop and attempt a jump-shot. If the coach remains silent the dribbler continues on with his dribble to the basket for a lay-up shot.

4:15 P.M. *Skeleton-plays drill.* (All players—no defense.)
4:20 P.M. *Half-court offensive work:*
> We free-lance and use plays against defensive players. The defense players will fast-break when they secure the ball and the offense players will try to break up the fast break. We make this practice now as much like a game as possible. Here, too, we will let the team that has been on defense and has secured the ball keep it until they get a good shot. Then we return to the half-court work. (To save time, set the

offense up at the defensive basket instead of returning to the other end of the court.)

4:55 P.M. *Passing and running drill with two balls—three men.*

5:00 P.M. *Free-throw shooting.* Eight (8) "one and one's."

PRACTICE 5

3:00 P.M. *All players jump rope for five (5) minutes.*

3:05 P.M. *Free shooting.* All players. (A ball for every player.)

3:10 P.M. *Passing drill.*

3:15 P.M. *Lay-up shooting practice.*

3:20 P.M. *Set-shooting (regular).*

3:25 P.M. *Jump-shots (three ball drill).*

3:30 P.M. *Fast-break.*

3:40 P.M. *"Give-and-Go" Practice:*

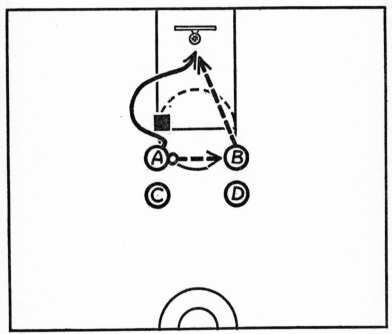

DIAGRAM 167. *"Push" Give-and-Go Drill.* A chair is placed on the floor
and two lines (one in front of the chair and the other to the left or right)
are formed. A player in the line in front of the chair passes to a player in
another line. The passer then goes to the basket and receives a return pass
for the shot. Note here the passer-cutter goes to the far side of the chair in
cutting for the basket. This is called the "push" give-and-go.

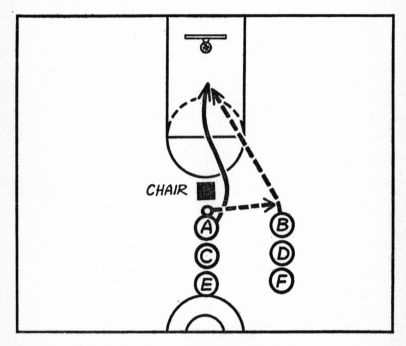

DIAGRAM 168. *"Regular" Give-and-Go Drill.* Here, the passer-cutter goes on the same side of the chair as his pass, and it is called the "regular" give-and-go.

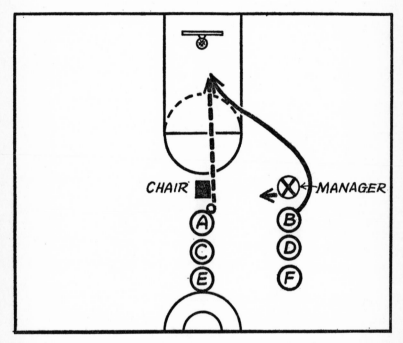

DIAGRAM 169. *"Sucker" Give-and-Go.* This diagram illustrates the give-and-go without the ball. When the manager (X) turns his head toward the player in front of the chair, the player on the sideline (in front of X) cuts for the basket and gets the ball from the passer (in the center of the court). (This drill is to press home the danger of turning the head when on the defense.)

3:50 P.M. *One-on-One.*

3:55 P.M. *Two-on-Two.*

Now, we stress not only screening and switching but the use of the give-and-go.

4:05 P.M. Breakdown drill feeding the pivot as described in previous material.

4:20 P.M. Half-court work. Here, the varsity (first eight players) goes on the defense and practices their fast-break when they succeed in getting the ball.

4:40 P.M. Passing and running drill—two balls and three men.

4:50 P.M. Free-throw practice.

While free-throw practice is going on, certain individuals will be told to practice certain weaknesses in

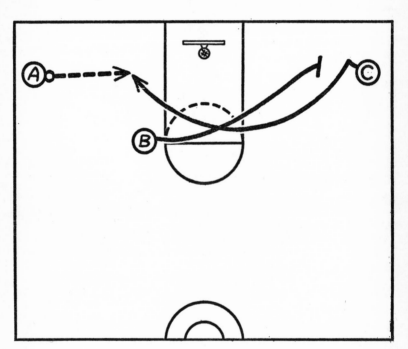

DIAGRAM 170. *Pivot Swinging.* The centers will make moves similar to those shown in this diagram to accustom themselves to "swinging" the pivot. Center (B) swings and screens for player (C) in the right corner. Player C cuts around the screen and to a pivot position on the left side of the lane where he receives the ball from A. The players are permitted to develop their own variations in this "swinging" of the pivot.

their play when they report the next day (before practice time if possible and during the free-shooting period if necessary). For example, centers will practice the following:

PRACTICE 6

3:00 P.M. *All players jump rope for five (5) minutes.*
3:05 P.M. *Free shooting.* All players. (A ball for every player.)
3:15 P.M. *Lay-up shooting drill.*
3:20 P.M. *Set-shooting.* Regular.
3:25 P.M. *Jump-shots* (three ball drill).
3:30 P.M. *Jump-ball practice* (groups of three).

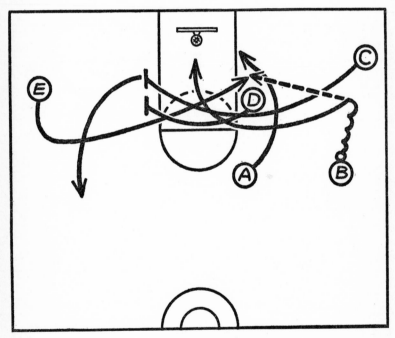

DIAGRAM 171. *Swinging the Pivot, Clear-outs and the Double Screen.* C clears across in front of pivot player D. As soon as he passes, D follows and joins C in setting up a double set-screen on the left side of the lane. B dribbles slowly to the right and passes the ball to teammate E who has cut behind the screen set by C and D. As soon as he passes the ball to E, B cuts as shown and A then cuts in front of E. This is one of our swing-pivot plays.

3:35 P.M. *Fast-break* (two men on defense).

3:50 P.M. *One-on-One.* (Use both ends of floor.)

3:55 P.M. *One-on-Two.* (Use both ends of floor.)

4:00 P.M. *Two-on-Two.* (Use both ends of floor.)

4:05 P.M. *Breakdown drill practice:*

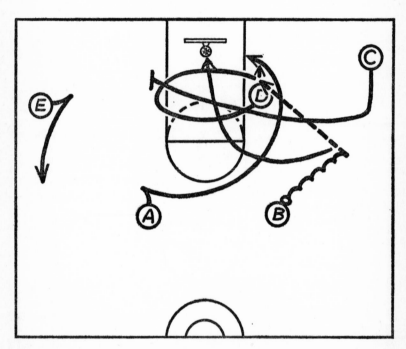

DIAGRAM 172. *"Come-back" Drill.* Player C starts a clearout by cutting across in front of D. Pivot man D starts as if to join C in setting up the double set-screen but circles back and receives the ball from B. After dribbling and passing to D, B cuts to the left and down the lane as in the preceding play. Player A cuts as before after faking to the left.

4:20 P.M. *Half floor offense.* Here, we start letting the players go a little further so that we are working semi-full floor work. We work first on offense and then on defense.

4:55 P.M. *Passing and running drill* (two balls—three men).

CHECK ALL PLAYERS FOR BLISTERS

PRACTICE 7

NOTE: On the days when we have full court scrimmages, we dispense with the hard-running drills as much as possible, so the players will not be tired out.

3:00 P.M. *All players jump rope for five (5) minutes.*

3:05 P.M. *Lay-up shooting drill.*

3:20 P.M. *Set-shooting in pairs.*

3:25 P.M. *Jump-shots* (stop and shoot drill).

3:30 P.M. *Rebound practice:*
1. Offensive
2. Defensive

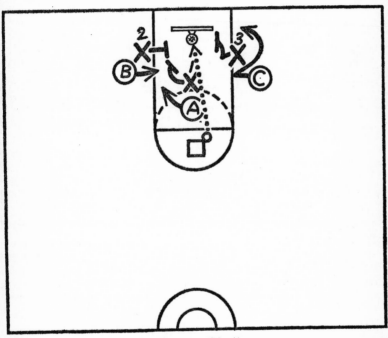

(Diagram 173–A)

(Diagram 173–B)

DIAGRAM 173. *Offensive and Defensive Rebounding.* In the drawing on the left ("A"), the coach shoots from the free-throw line and A, B, and C follow-in. Defensive players X-1, X-2, and X-3 block out. In the drawing on the right ("B"), the offensive players take different attacking positions. Here, the accent is on defensive blocking-out and rebounding.

3:45 P.M. Half-court offensive and defensive practice.

4:00 P.M. Full-court scrimmage under game conditions. Managers keep charts on shooting, passing, rebounding, assists. This scrimmage is restricted to man-to-man defensive work. (Remember to work your first eight men together and never against one another. Substitute your first eight men freely.) Talk to players who come out regarding mistakes, oversights, missed plays, etc.

PRACTICE 8

3:00 P.M. *All players jump rope for five (5) minutes.*

3:05 P.M. *Free shooting.* All players. (A ball for every player.)

3:15 P.M. *Discuss the previous day's scrimmage.* Demonstrate with players on the floor mistakes, missed plays, defensive oversights, etc.

LOTS OF FUNDAMENTAL WORK TODAY

3:30 P.M. *Lay-up shooting drill.*

3:35 P.M. *Set-shots.* Regular.

3:40 P.M. *Jump-shots.* (Three balls.)

3:45 P.M. *Fast-break.* Two men on defense.

3:55 P.M. *One-on-One.*

4:00 P.M. *One-on-Two.*

4:05 P.M. *Two-on-Two practice:*

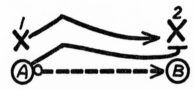

DIAGRAM 174. *Offensive Block-Off for Shots.* Here, we will stress blocking-off for set-shots as well as defense against blocking-off. Players work in groups of four. (A) passes to B and blocks-off for him. Defensive player X-1 moves with him and when A stops immediately executes a "crotch." (See next diagram.)

DIAGRAM 175. *"Crotch" and Switch Drill.* A "crotch" move is made when the defensive player (X-1) places his left foot between the legs of A and plants his right foot halfway between B and A as shown above. Defensive player X-1 also places his left arm close to the chest of A. Defensive player X-1 will now try to force B to make his move. Whatever A and B now do, defensive players X-1 and X-2 will switch as shown. If A and B go the same direction, the front defensive player will take the front offensive player and the back defensive player will take the back offensive player. Should B go to *his* right, X-2 will guard him and X-1 will remain with A. Should player B go to *his* left, defensive player X-1 will take him and defensive player X-2 will guard A. No matter which way the offensive players go, they are covered quickly and efficiently. (This defensive maneuver requires plenty of practice.)

4:25 P.M. *Run Skeleton Plays.* Players are not yet sure of execution.

4:45 P.M. *Rebound drill.* Now, we practice the fast-break from the rebound drill.

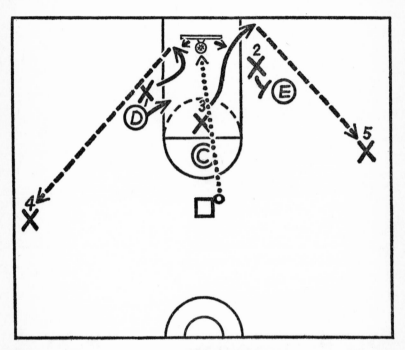

DIAGRAM 176. *Rebound and Fast Break Drill.*   Here, we are playing three offense players (C, D, and E) against three defense players (X-1, X-2, and X-3). The basket is covered and the coach shoots. If a defense player secures the rebound, he immediately hits a lay-out man (X-4 or X-5) and the fast break is started. The purpose of this drill is to get the rebound men in the habit of hitting their lay-out teammates as soon as they secure the ball.

5:00 P.M. *Passing and running drill* (two balls and three men).

5:10 P.M. *Free-throw shooting.*

(We have purposefully eliminated half-court and scrimmage work so the players will look forward to this type of practice.)

16

Practice Sessions
Nine Through Fifteen

PRACTICE 9

3:00 P.M. *Free shooting.* All players. (A ball for every player.)

3:15 P.M. *Lay-up shooting drill.*

3:20 P.M. *Set-shots.* Regular.

3:25 P.M. *Jump-shots.* Three balls.

3:30 P.M. *Fast Break.* Two men on defense.

3:45 P.M. *One-on-One.*

3:50 P.M. *One-on-Two.*

3:55 P.M. *Two-on-Two.*

4:00 P.M. *Reverse Cutting Practice:*

4:05 P.M. *Half-court defense and fast-break.* (We start with "clear-outs" and "cut-backs" and then work into all plays.) This work is at full speed. . . .

4:35 P.M. *Full court scrimmage.* Charts are kept listing shots taken and made, assists, bad passes, rebounds, etc. (At this time, your chart manager can begin to keep statistics on the success or failure of the various play combinations.)

4:50 P.M. *Passing and running drill.* (Two balls and three men.)

5:00 P.M. *Free-throw practice.*

Now is the time to give some extra attention to those players who have not been able to get out to practice on time, or who have been sidelined because of an injury or an illness. Check their shots, and other

235

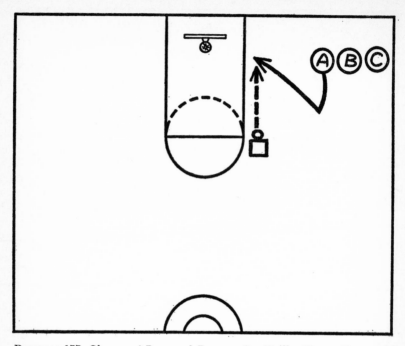

DIAGRAM 177. *Change of Pace and Reverse Cut Drill.* Players line up in the corner. Each, in turn, starts leisurely for the back court and then suddenly reverses toward the basket and cuts at full speed for the ball. The coach can vary his passes (baseball—bounce—two-hand overhead—underhand flip, etc.).

fundamentals and clear up their uncertainties regarding the offenses or defenses (use blackboard). Players who have reported late are now required to complete their rope jumping.

PRACTICE 10

3:00 P.M. *All players jump rope for five (5) minutes.* (Rope jumping is now given on alternate days.)

3:05 P.M. *Lay-up shooting practice:*

3:20 P.M. *Set-shots.* In pairs.

3:25 P.M. *Jump-shots.* Three balls.

3:30 P.M. *Fast-break.* Today we will make sure the lay-out player keeps the ball once in a while instead of always passing to the middle man on the break.

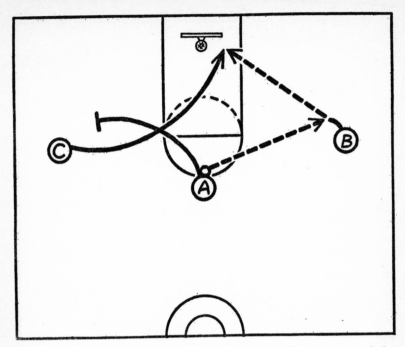

DIAGRAM 178. *"V" and Screen Drill.* This change in execution of the lay-up drill is to bring something new to the players and yet accomplish the desired result. Here, the players develop the habit of screening "away" following a pass to a teammate. Screening away practice firms up the idea of setting a screen for a teammate (doing something when he does not have the ball).

3:45 P.M. *One-on-One.*

3:50 P.M. *Two-on-Two.*

3:55 P.M. *Work on Three-Out—Two-In Offense.* Skeleton weave as outlined in previous material. Here, we work only on the weave. No plays! The weave is important to our "set" offense because everything we do starts with a weave.

4:15 P.M. *Three Out—Two-In weave against man-to-man defense.* No plays! Since the weave as we use it involves "down the middle" and "give-and-go" features, it is vital that our players master the weave to perfection.

4:25 P.M. *Skeleton and slow motion practice.* Three-Out—Two-

In offense on floor, and check it against plays on blackboard. Explain all uncertainties.

4:40 P.M. *Skeleton run at full speed of all Three-Out—Two-In plays.* Use defense.

4:55 P.M. *Passing and Running Drill* (two balls and three men).

5:00 P.M. *Free-throw shooting.*

PRACTICE 11

(NO ROPE JUMPING TODAY)

3:00 P.M. *Free shooting.* All players. (A ball for every player.)

3:15 P.M. *Lay-up shooting.* "Screen Away."

3:20 P.M. *Set-shot practice.* In pairs.

DIAGRAM 179. *Two-Man Recover and Shoot Drill.* Player A shoots, recovers the ball, passes it back to teammate B, and returns to the back court. B now shoots, recovers the ball and passes back to A. This alternate shooting, recovering, and passing back continues until one player makes twenty (20) points.

3:25 P.M. *Jump-shots.* Stop and shoot.

3:30 P.M. *Fast-break.* Two men on defense.

3:45 P.M. *Two-on-Two.*

3:55 P.M. *Breakdown drill feeding pivot on pivot offense.*

4:05 P.M. *Half-court set-up of pivot offense with defense fast-breaking.*

4:20 P.M. *Half-court set-up of Three-Out—Two-In.* Full speed against man-to-man defense and with defense team using fast-break.

4:35 P.M. *Full-court scrimmage.* Pivot offense, ten minutes. Three-Out—Two-In, ten minutes.

4:55 P.M. *Passing and running drill.* Two balls and three men.

5:00 P.M. *Free-throw practice.*

PRACTICE 12

3:00 P.M. *All players jump rope for five (5) minutes.*

3:05 P.M. *Free shooting.* All players. (A ball for every player.)

3:15 P.M. *Lay-up shots.* Regular.

3:20 P.M. *Set-shots.* Regular.

3:25 P.M. *Jump-shots.* Three balls.

3:30 P.M. *Fast-break.*

3:45 P.M. *One-on-One.*

3:50 P.M. *One-on-Two.*

3:55 P.M. *Two-on-Two.*

4:00 P.M. *Rebound offensive and defensive.* Use fast-break from defensive rebound. Five against three.

4:10 P.M. *Run skeleton plays of Three-Out—Two-In Offense.*

4:20 P.M. *Half-court practice on both offenses with defensive team using fast break.* Varsity will work half of this period on defense.

4:40 P.M. *Scrimmage.* Entire court. Simulate game conditions.

5:00 P.M. *Passing and running drill.* Three balls and two men.

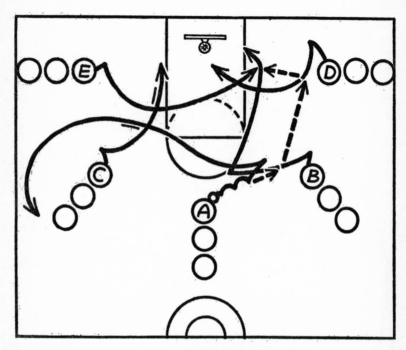

DIAGRAM 180. *Skeleton Offense Drill.* The Three-Two offense is being used and each team runs through a Three-Two play. Here, A passes to B and executes the V. Player B passes to D and changes direction to cut past E who has been screened by C. Player D passes to E and cuts off the pivot.

CHECK FREE-THROW SHOOTING

PRACTICE 13

Today, we scrimmage the freshmen under game conditions. Officials, time-outs, substitutions, everything. . . . (No rope-skipping today.)

3:00 P.M. *Pre-game warm-up:*

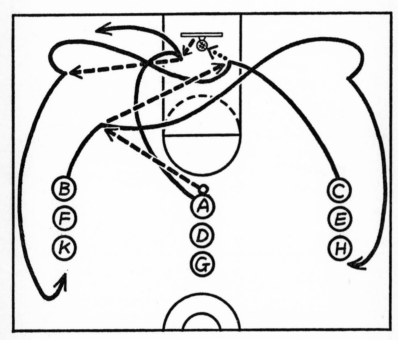

DIAGRAM 181. *Warm-up Drill.* Two balls are used in this drill. The players form three lines and pass as shown. The ball is passed from A to B to C. Player C shoots and goes to the corner. B does likewise. Player A rebounds and passes the ball to either teammate.

3:20 P.M. *Scrimmage game.* During the first half we will play a standard game observing everything necessary to simulate actual game. The second half will be devoted to a look at our second and third units and other prospects.

PRACTICE 14

3:00 P.M. *All players jump rope for five (5) minutes.*

3:05 P.M. *Free shooting.* All players. (A ball for every player.)

3:15 P.M. *Discussion of yesterday's scrimmage with freshmen.*
Corrections and uncertainties ironed out.

3:25 P.M. *Lay-up shooting.*

3:30 P.M. *Set-shots.* Regular.

3:35 P.M. *Jump-shots.* Three balls.

3:40 P.M. *Fast-break.* Two men on defense.

3:55 P.M. *One-on-One.*

4:05 P.M. *One-on-Two.*

4:15 P.M. *Two-on-Two.*

4:25 P.M. *Break-down Drills:*
1. Clear-outs and comebacks.

DIAGRAM 182. *Corner Clear-Out Drill.* The diagram on the left shows a "straight" clear-out. The diagram on the right shows a "screen and reverse" corner clear-out.

4:25 P.M. Cont'd

    2. Feeding high post pivot.

    3. Feeding regular pivot.

    4. Work on "flood" play. Stress give-and-go play from Three-Out—Two-In offense.

4:45 P.M. Half-court, working on material covered in breakdown drill of Three-Out—Two-In offense.

5:00 P.M. Passing and Running Drill. Two balls and three men.

FREE-THROW SHOOTING

PRACTICE 15

NO ROPE JUMPING TODAY

3:00 P.M. *Free shooting.* All players. (A ball for every player.)

3:15 P.M. *Lay-up shots.*

3:20 P.M. *Set-shots.*

3:25 P.M. *Jump-shots.* Three balls.

3:30 P.M. *Fast break.* Two men on defense.

3:45 P.M. *One-on-One.*

3:50 P.M. *Work half-court on Three-Out—Two-In offense only.* No pivot offense today. I want to improve ball handling and moves and this offense requires it.

4:20 P.M. *Defensive zone practice.* The Two-One-Two and the One-Two-Two zones are now developed. No offense is used. Player A moves to various spots on the floor and the defensive players make the correct defensive zone moves. The following diagrams illustrate some of the moves:

DIAGRAM 183. *Starting Position of the Dartmouth Two-One-Two zone with the ball at "A".*

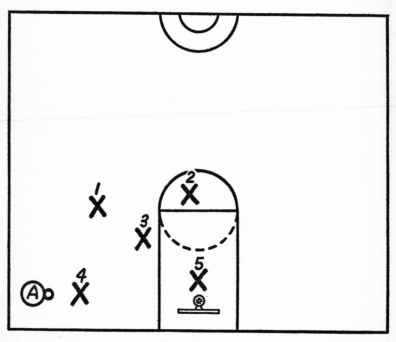

DIAGRAM 184. *Two-One-Two Zone Slides.* Ball is at position "A".

DIAGRAM 185. *"Triple-up" Drill.* Chasers 1 and 2 combine here with teammate 3 in trying to tie up the ball.

DIAGRAM 186. *Two-One-Two Zone Slides.* With the ball in the corner in the possession of D, the above slides are made by the defensive players.

245

DIAGRAM 187. *Starting position of the One-Two-Two Zone.* With the ball at "A", the One-Two-Two forms as shown.

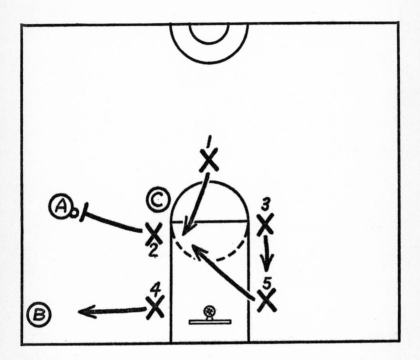

DIAGRAM 188. *One-Two-Two Zone Slides.* The slides shown above are consistent and are always the same on either side of the court (depending upon the movement of the ball).

4:40 P.M. *Zone attack against our zone defenses:* This offense has been previously described. The fast-break must be defensed when the zone players secure the ball.

4:55 P.M. *Passing and running drill.* Two balls and three men.

FREE-THROW SHOOTING

17

Practice Sessions Sixteen Through Twenty-Six

So far, we have practiced only on week days (Monday through Friday). Now, we will work on Saturdays when possible, once in the morning for an hour on our fundamentals, offenses and defenses and then again in the afternoon when we will stage a game (simulated).

PRACTICE 16

MORNING PRACTICE:

10:00 A.M. *All players jump rope for five (5) minutes.*
10:05 A.M. *Free shooting.* All players. (A ball for every man.)
10:15 A.M. *Jump-shots.*
10:20 A.M. *Set-shots.*
10:25 A.M. *Fast break.*
10:30 A.M. *Half-court zone defenses.* (Two-One-Two and One-Two-Two.)
10:45 A.M. *Half-court zone attacks.*

11:00 A.M. *Passing and running drill.* Two balls and three men.

FREE-THROW SHOOTING

AFTERNOON PRACTICE:
3:00 P.M. *Pre-Game Warm-Up.*
3:20 P.M. *Formal scrimmage game.* Outside team if possible.

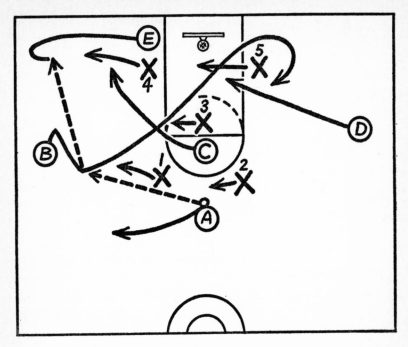

DIAGRAM 189. *Zone Attack Drill.* This practice time will be devoted to setting up our zone attacks against the Two-One-Two, One-Two-Two, and One-Three-One zone defenses. In the above One-Three-One attack against a Two-One-Two zone defense, Player A starts the attack by passing to B and covering. B passes to E and cuts through the zone. If no play is made, D replaces B by driving into the same area by way of the lane. C has also cut and will replace E. E, with the ball, will feed B, D, or C or return the ball to the back court and replace C on the free-throw line. The cutting may be used on either side of the court.

Here, we use all our offensive measures, defensive styles, and practice certain game strategy.

4:30 P.M. *End of practice for week.* Coach will go to dressing room and talk with players. Try to give them a lift. Use a lot of praise. Send them away from the long grind they have passed through with a smile.

PRACTICE 17

3:00 P.M. *All players jump rope for five (5) minutes.*

3:05 P.M. *Free shooting.* All players. (A ball for every man.)

3:15 P.M. *Set shots*. In pairs.
3:20 P.M. *Lay-up shooting*.
3:25 P.M. *Jump-shots*. Three balls.
3:30 P.M. *Fast-break*.
3:45 P.M. *One-on-One*.
3:50 P.M. *One-on-Two*.
3:55 P.M. *Two-on-Two*.
4:00 P.M. *Pivot break-down drill*.
4:10 P.M. *Three-Out—Two-In break-down drill*.
4:20 P.M. *Work on plays versus the zone defenses:*
    1. Continuity.
    2. Fake and drive.
4:40 P.M. *Full court scrimmage*. Use all three offenses from time to time by shifting on signal from one to the other. Instruct defensive team to also shift from man-to-man defense to the zone defenses without advising attack-

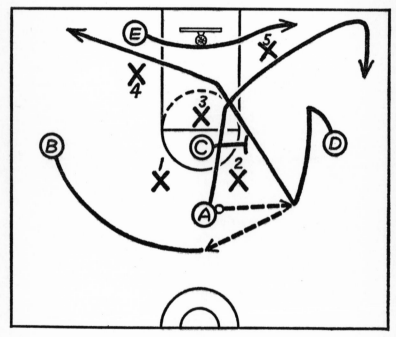

DIAGRAM 190. *Meeting Aggressive Zone Chasers.* The position-changes shown here are practiced to teach our back court players to move so the defensive chasers will be kept off balance.

ing team. (The players will look ragged in this work since it is the first time they have combined all offenses and defenses.)

5:10 P.M. *Passing and running drill:*

PRACTICE 18

NO ROPE JUMPING TODAY

3:00 P.M. *Free shooting.* All players. (A ball for every player.) (Players often report early for practice. After they have completed their rope jumping, they work on their weaknesses, attempting certain shots, dribbling, rebounding, getting position, tapping ball in basket on missed shots, special work on One-on-One, etc. The coach should supervise this individual work and

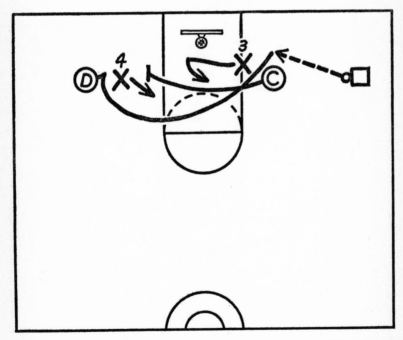

DIAGRAM 191. *Pivot Change Drill.* In this drill, players C and D exchange positions and try to get clear for a pass. The coach passes the ball if the player gets good position on the lane.

make sure that the pre-practice and free shooting time is spent in serious work.

3:15 P.M. *Lay-up shooting.*

3:25 P.M. *Set-shots.* Regular.

3:35 P.M. *Pivot Interchange:*

3:45 P.M. *Fast-break.* Two men on defense.

4:00 P.M. *One-on-One.*

4:10 P.M. *Scrimmage.* All offenses and defenses. Varsity on offense twenty minutes and on defense twenty minutes.

4:50 P.M. *Passing and running drill.* Two balls and three men.

4:55 P.M. *Free-throw practice.*

NOTE: The squad has now advanced to the point where offense and defense auxiliary work, held ball formations, out-of-bounds plays, the press, and other advanced work may be practiced.

PRACTICE 19

3:00 P.M. *All players jump rope for five (5) minutes.*

3:05 P.M. *Lay-up shooting.*

3:10 P.M. *Set-shots.*

3:15 P.M. *Jump-shots.* Three balls.

3:20 P.M. *Fast-break.*

3:35 P.M. *One-on-One.*

3:40 P.M. *One-on-Two.*

3:45 P.M. *Two-on-Two.*

3:50 P.M. *Break-down drill:*

4:10 P.M. *Special practice on the man-to-man press and the zone press as previously described.* Special work on how to come out of the press.

4:30 P.M. *Held-ball plays in all three circles.*

4:45 P.M. *Out-of-bounds plays.* Side and end of court.

5:00 P.M. *Passing and shooting drill.* Two balls and three men.

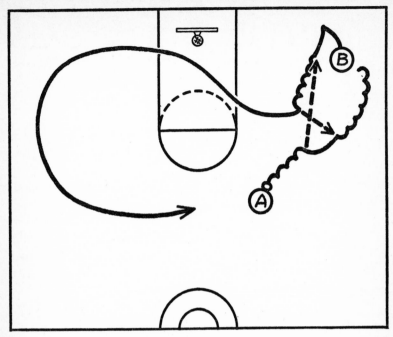

DIAGRAM 192. *Screening Out of Corner.* Here, offense players A and B are employing give-and-go and corner clear-out tactics to break free for a shot. These screens, naturally, should be practiced from both sides of the court. All moves are practiced in which a back court man and a corner man can screen and exchange places.

FREE-THROW PRACTICE

PRACTICE 20

This is Thanksgiving Day and we will work for one hour in the morning and hold a scrimmage game with an outside team or the freshman team in the afternoon. It is important that we play against a strong team if such a scrimmage is possible.

MORNING PRACTICE:

NO ROPE JUMPING TODAY

10:00 A.M. *Free shooting.*
10:15 A.M. *This period will be spent in review of the man-to-*

man and the zone presses; coming out of both types of press; jump balls; out-of-bounds plays; the offenses and the defenses; and any phase of our game which may not be clear to the players.

10:55 A.M. *Free-throw shooting.*

AFTERNOON PRACTICE:

3:00 P.M. *Pre-game warm-up.*

3:20 P.M. *Scrimmage with strong outside team under full game conditions.* In this scrimmage game we attempt to try out our special strategy plays such as "freezing" the ball; using the possession attack; playing for one shot; shifting our attack and defense, etc. After the first eight or nine players have played two halves, we try to play a third half so that our second and third teams may get a work-out. It may be that some player whom we have counted on as a first string man may be a "practice" player, and one of the men we had regarded as second or third string prove to be a sleeper (excels when the pressure is on in game conditions).

PRACTICE 21

This is the day after Thanksgiving and we will plan for two practice sessions. We will work lightly in the morning and hit it hard in the afternoon.

MORNING PRACTICE:

10:00 A.M. *A meeting is held at which the blackboard and the floor are used to review the previous day's scrimmage game.* All phases of the game will be discussed: Bad shots, poor passes, weak blocking-out efforts, lack of follow-in tactics, poor execution of plays, weak defensive moves, failure to talk on the defense, poor switching, etc.

10:30 A.M. *A movie will be shown of one of last year's games in which we looked good on the offense.* Then we will show a game in which we looked good on defense. While we are showing the films, I will discuss the good and the bad plays and reverse the films to slow motion speed so that the points may be stressed and (it is hoped) remembered.

11:00 A.M. *Free shooting.*

11:10 A.M. *Three-man basketball.* The players are assigned to three-man teams and play elimination games. During this practice, players who are not playing watch the game on the floor. At this time we want to encourage team spirit and "fun."

AFTERNOON PRACTICE:

3:00 P.M. *Rope jumping by all players for five (5) minutes.*

3:05 P.M. *Lay-up shooting.*

3:10 P.M. *Set-shots.*

3:15 P.M. *Jump-shots.* Three balls.

3:20 P.M. *Fast break.*

3:40 P.M. *One-on-One.*

3:45 P.M. *One-on-Two.*

3:50 P.M. *Two-on-Two.*

3:55 P.M. *Dribble show!* Each player takes a ball and warms up by dribbling behind his back, between his legs (forward and backward), while on his knees, etc. At the end, in order to get some team enthusiasm, we select the best "show" dribblers (two or three) and let their teammates choose the player who puts on the best show by their applause.

4:10 P.M. *Half-court pivot offense:*

1. Varsity take the defense and fast break when they get the ball.

2. Three-Out—Two-In. Same as above.

3. Zone attack. Same as above.

(In this work we change off so that each group gets plenty of work on the offense as well as the defense.)

4:45 P.M. *Special work on out-of-bounds plays and "one shot" plays.*

4:55 P.M. *Special work on semi-freeze, full freeze, and possession attack.*

5:15 P.M. *Passing and running drill.* Two balls and three men.

FREE-THROW PRACTICE

(We will have one or two days off now until the Thanksgiving vacation is finished. Here we all heave a sigh of relief. The nose grinding is mostly over. This is the time to "whoop it up!")

PRACTICE 22

NO ROPE JUMPING TODAY

(FIRST GAME FIVE DAYS AWAY)
"Break in game shoes"

3:00 P.M. *Free shooting.*

3:15 P.M. *Lay-up shooting.*

3:20 P.M. *Set-shots.*

3:25 P.M. *Jump-shots.* Three balls.

3:30 P.M. *Fast-break.* Two men on defense.

3:45 P.M. *One-on-One.*

3:50 P.M. *One-on-Two.*

3:55 P.M. *Two-on-Two.* (Stress coming out of corners.)

4:00 P.M. *Rebounding.* (Offense and defense.)
Five against three practicing fast break.

4:10 P.M. *Half-court work on all offensive plays.* Defensive players fast break. Defense must hold on to ball for a good shot if they do not have a good fast-break shot. As soon as they get the shot, stop the action and start over again. Gradually ease into a full court scrimmage by allowing the defense to keep the ball longer each time. Use all offenses and all defenses. (Each team changes its offense or defense at any time without letting other team know.)

4:55 P.M. *Passing and shooting drill.* Two balls and three men.

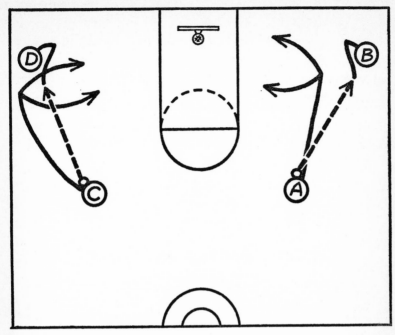

DIAGRAM 193. *To Corner-and-Out Drill.* On the left, player C passes to D and cuts behind him. When D does not return the ball, C cuts left or right and looks for a return pass. On the right, player A passes to B and sets a screen. When B does not dribble or pass to another teammate, (A) cuts left or right and looks for a return pass.

FREE-THROW PRACTICE

PRACTICE 23

3:00 P.M. *All players jump rope five (5) minutes.*

3:05 P.M. *Free shooting.* Here again, players work on weak shots, dribbling, rebounding, tapping-in shots. Coach should make these assignments.

3:20 P.M. *Lay-up shots.* Players count and try to break consecutive lay-up shot record.

3:30 P.M. *Set-shots in pairs.* Check for best shooting pair.

3:35 P.M. *Jump-shots.* Three balls. Check for record on number of shots made out of fifty (50) and number of consecutive shots.

3:45 P.M. *Fast-break.*

3:55 P.M. *One-on-One.* Stress drive from sides of court.

4:00 P.M. *One-on-Two.* Make defensive man work hard.

4:05 P.M. *Two-on-Two.* Practice:

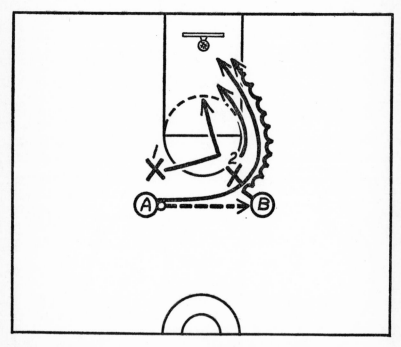

DIAGRAM 194. *Trailer Drill.* This is a good move. Player A passes to B and cross-screens. Defensive players X-1 and X-2 are expecting an ordinary cross screen and call "switch!" but do not move in with their men. Player B (now with the ball) fakes to cross screen but, instead, dribbles behind the screener (A). A good two-on-one situation is possible here.

4:15 P.M. *Two-on-two blocking-off for set shots and defense against it.* Described earlier. This is important to our defense. In moving rapidly on the weave the players have not demonstrated that they can block-off well for a teammate's set-shot and are not even faking the blocking-off of a set-shot. *This must be corrected now!*

4:25 P.M. *Run skeleton plays from all offenses.* No defense. Cover every play and variation.

4:30 P.M. *Half-court work stressing pivot man getting into position and swinging the pivot.*

4:50 P.M. *Half-court Three-Out—Two-In offense.* Stress starting all plays from the weave.

5:00 P.M. *Work against the man-to-man and the zone press.*

5:15 P.M. *Passing and shooting drill.* Two balls and three men.

FREE SHOOTING PRACTICE

NOTE: From now on we will start to taper off. We want our players to have their legs under them by Saturday.

PRACTICE 24

Today we scrimmage the freshman team in a game dress rehearsal. Game uniforms, officials, play the clock, bench proce-

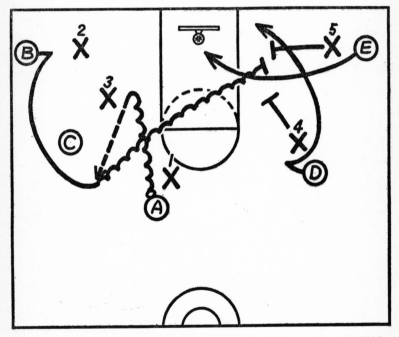

DIAGRAM 195. *Meeting the Sag and the Float.* Attacking player A dribbles to a set screen position behind opponent X-3. Teammate C will hold his position so B can cut around the screen and receive the ball from A. B will now dribble to a position behind opponents X-5 or X-4 and E or D will break for the basket.

dure and strategy, all offenses and defenses, the freeze, ball control, playing for one shot, etc.

3:00 P.M. *Pre-game warm-up.*

3:20 P.M. *Regulation game with freshmen.*

> In this game the freshmen will use sagging and floating tactics. The varsity will meet these with the "one-on-one" and "two-on-two" as well as moving and set screens directed toward the sagger and floater. The following principle will be stressed.

PRACTICE 25

3:00 P.M. *All players jump rope for five (5) minutes.*

3:05 P.M. *Free shooting.* All players. A ball for every player.

3:15 P.M. *Lay-up shooting.*

3:20 P.M. *Set-shots.* Regular.

3:25 P.M. *Jump-shots.* Three balls.

3:30 P.M. *Fast-break.*

3:45 P.M. *One-on-One.*

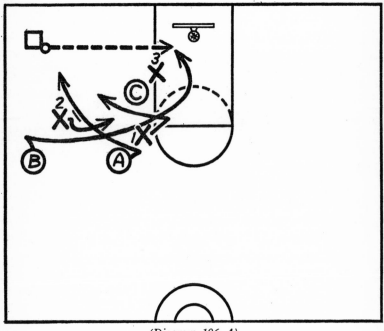

(Diagram 196–A)

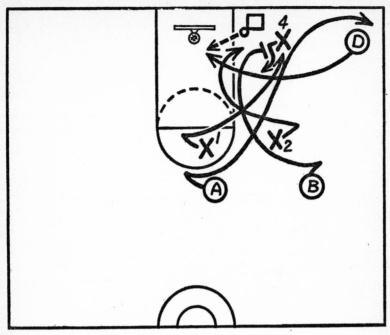

(Diagram 196–B)

DIAGRAM 196. *Screen and Slice Drills.* The coach takes a position on the base line with the ball and the players use various screens and slicing plays to break a teammate free. In diagram A, A screens for B to give him a chance to cut for the basket. In diagram B, A again screens for B. This time, however, B sets a screen behind D's opponent (X-4) and D uses A and B to break loose.

3:50 P.M. *One-on-Two.*

3:55 P.M. *Two-on-Two.*

4:00 P.M. *Work on held-ball situations.*
Work on out-of-bounds plays.
Work on one-shot plays.

4:20 P.M. *Since you do not know what your opening-game opponent will use offensively or defensively, work against all defenses:* man-to-man; zone; zone press; man-to-man press.

4:40 P.M. *Sharpen up all offenses with half-court floor work.* Defense fast-break.

5:00 P.M. *Screening and Cutting Practice:*

Practice 26

DAY BEFORE OPENING GAME

3:00 P.M. *Free shooting.* A ball for every player.

3:20 P.M. *Lay-up shooting.*

3:25 P.M. *Set-shots.*

3:30 P.M. *Jump shots.*

3:35 P.M. *Ten minutes of scrimmage against man-to-man defense.* An all-out practice.

3:45 P.M. *Passing and running drill.* Two balls and three men.

3:55 P.M. *Use the court and the blackboard to run through the Coach's offense and defense check lists.* Players should quickly demonstrate every item on the list.

18

In-Season Practices, Coaching Review, Scouting Reports

In-season practice sessions will, naturally, be built around the game schedule and school holidays. The coach will want to add plays and defenses to keep team interest and considerable time will be spent getting ready for key opponents. However, a skeleton form covering a two hour practice session should be prepared and used as a guide. At Dartmouth we cut down practice periods and cut down on the time about fifteen minutes. First, we break our two hour period up into fifteen (15) minute periods. Two fifteen minute periods can be spent on one phase of the game. In the following schedule, each number covers approximately fifteen minutes.

1. Discuss pro & con the previous night's ball game:
   a. Read off the team statistics of the game
   b. Correct mistakes
   c. Be sure to discuss what they did well
   d. Have them ask questions
   e. Use the last minute of this discussion to tell them that last night's game is history; we must start getting ready for the next one.
2. Jump rope and shooting on their own:
   Each player works on his weakness, trying a new shot, etc.

Anything which might help him is recommended

3. Regular shooting practice:
    a. Lay-ups
    b. Set-shots   (These should be varied so the players
    c. Jump-shots   will get practice in *all* shots *every* day.)
4. Fast break:
    a. Skeleton
    b. With two men on defense
    c. Fast-break from rebound (five versus three).
    NOTE: Do not practice rebound fast-break every day.
5. Fundamentals:
    a. One-on-one every day
    b. One-on-two (alternate days)
    c. Two-on-two (alternate days)
    d. Breakdown drills in place of a, b, and c.
6. Work on defense for next game:
    a. Practice your man-to-man defense against opponents'
       pet plays and moves.
          Decide how much switching you are going to do and
          practice it.
    b. Set up your zone defenses against opponents' zone attack
       1. Decide which of your zone defenses will work best.
          Stress it more.
       2. Make adjustments to meet the opponents' style of
          play.
    c. Your combination defense:
       1. If you are going to use a combination defense, it is
          suggested that you do not use it against a weak team.
       2. Practice your man-to-man and zone press.
          NOTE: You cannot do this all in fifteen minutes in a
          given day. What you did not do today—be sure to do
          tomorrow.
7 and 8. Work on your own offense:
    a. Pivot if you think it best
    b. Three-Two attack for a change of pace
    c. Zone attack:
          Have your reserves use various zones so you are
          prepared for any type.

d. Coming out of the man-to-man and the zone presses:
You should know from your scouting reports which
type of zone opponents use best.

During these last two periods you can use half-court techniques as well as the whole floor. We do some of each. Here,
too, you can practice stopping the opponents' fast break
(especially when you are working half-floor set-ups). Practice
your offensive work against the fast-break defense at the same
time.

9. Windup: Running and passing with three men and two
   balls.

FREE-THROWS

COACHING REVIEW

During your preparation for the first game, you must make
sure that you have covered everything in offense and defense.
Be sure your team is fully prepared to cope with any offense,
defense, or strategical move your opponents may use. So, starting about a week before your opening game, sit down and
make up a list. "Have I covered everything in our *offense?*"

1. Pivot Offense
2. Three-Two
3. Advancing ball safely
4. Fast break
5. Jump balls:
   a. At center circle
   b. Front court
   c. Rear court
6. Attacking zone:
   a. Two-One-Two
   b. One-Two-Two
   c. One-Three-One
7. Coming out of the man-to-man press
8. Coming out of zone presses (2-2-1) (3-1-1) (1-2-2)
9. Out-of-bounds plays:
   a. At end
   b. At side

10. One-shot plays:
  a. Against man-to-man defense
  b. Against zone defenses
11. Semi-freeze
12. Attacking sagging and floating
13. Freezing
14. Possession of Ball
15. Meeting screen-switch defense
16. Meeting combination defenses.

"Have I covered everything in our *defense?*"
1. Man-to-man defense (normal):
  a. Front-slide-switch
  b. Block-out
  c. Rebound
2. Sagging, Floating, Overshifting
3. Switching man-to-man
4. Zone defenses:
  a. Two-One-Two
  b. One-Two-Two
  c. One-Three-One
5. Defense against opponents' tap
6. Defense against the fast-break
7. Man-to-man press
8. Zone press
9. Combination defenses of man-to-man and zone.

ACTUAL SCOUTING REPORTS

The scouting reports which follow are those we have used during the past several years. They are presented here so you may see exactly what we expect from our scouts. We go over the respective report several times with our players, using the blackboard to stress important points. After each "skull" session, we go out on the floor and repeat the same points "on the court" so our players may get a "game" picture of our opponents' moves.

In discussing individual opponents, I often say: "Play him *one* arm away, or *two* arms away, or *three* arms away." One night we were playing Princeton in an important game and one of their players had not shown up in our scouting reports as much of a player. So I told one of my boys to stay "three arms" away from him. At the half, the Princeton "poor shooter" had fourteen points! "The best laid plans of mice and men. . . ."

WEST VIRGINIA SCOUTING REPORT

Defense: Against WV, Canisius used the weave with WV naturally playing man for man. They pressed all the way from the time the ball was taken out of bounds. Each man pressing his own man. The press itself was not that effective and seemed to be wide open for *mistakes.* By that we mean, had the man passing the ball followed the pass, Canisius could have used the give and go very effectively, because WV did not charge the ball, they just tried to lead Canisius into mistakes and slow the ball down.

I believe the main purpose of the WV press was to keep the weave pushed out away from the key and it did exactly that.

If Canisius did manage to move the ball in close, WV would switch and without hesitation move out and pick up. They did this very effectively. Even when a good screen was set up one man would always go out and get the ball. This did leave opportunities for the give and go but I don't feel Canisius took advantage of this.

On this, I can suggest two things (1) Using the give and go when WV does switch—or (2) using the give and go away on the weave.

Starting Lineup:

RG	30	Bolyard	5'11	185	Right Hand Shot
LG	21	Smith	6'4	185	Right Hand Shot
C	34	Clousson	6'6	200	Right Hand Shot
RF	32	Akers	6'5	195	Left Hand Shot
LF	44	West	6'3	175	Right Hand Shot
6th Man	25	Posch for Clousson			
			6'7	205	
7th Man	35	Ritchie for Akers			
			6'5	185	

Opening Tap: Clousson tapped forward to West.

Offense: Against WV, Canisius used a 2-3 zone on defense. WV set up their offense with a 1-3-1 set up.

Bolyard out in front feeding West and Smith on the sides, Clousson on the foul line and Akers underneath. Akers would be on the side the ball would be on.

Note: Forgot to mention that they didn't move back on defense real fast but Canisius didn't fast break but once or twice the whole night. So if you did fast break I can't really say whether or not they would get back fast enough but they are fast enough to do so. There isn't a single man on their club who can't move well.

Back to the offense: They make great use of the man on the key. Against the zone they move the ball real fast trying to pull the back line away for Clousson. Then they would hit him. If he was open he took the shot but he was very good at hitting West and Smith on the sides.

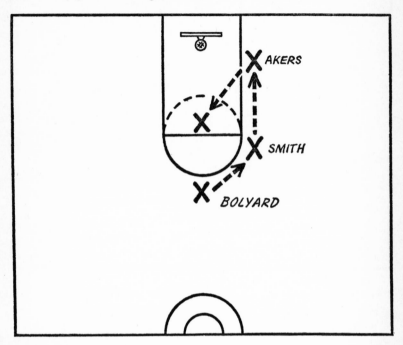

Bolyard would hit Smith, Smith to Akers, Akers to Clousson. They moved the ball real fast on this and before the forward, who covered Smith when he got the ball, could get back to block off Clousson, Clousson had the ball. I know if you don't use a zone against them this report may not be the best but if you do, your men will have to recover fast once they've made move.

Sometimes they would set up with a 1-2-2 offense with both Akers and Clousson underneath. One of the two would move out to the line fast. Bolyard would hit him with the ball and he would then hit the man on the side before the forward recovers.

On the first play, Bolyard threw a high pass from the top of the key to Akers directly under the basket. Akers leaped for it, came down, then laid it up and in.

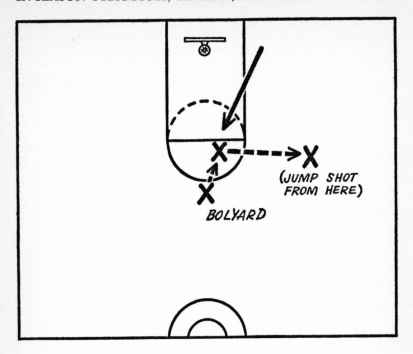

Here, Bolyard hit Clousson from the middle and Clousson would pass quickly to West or Smith at "x" for a quick jumper.

Another play they used against the zone:

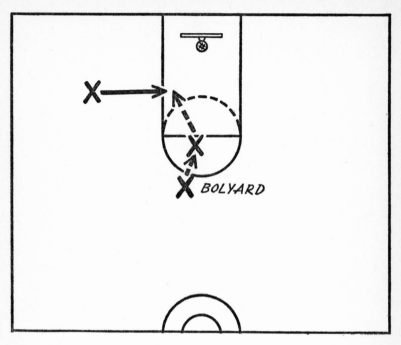

Bolyard hit the center and at the same time, the man underneath came across the key from the side of the key. The center would turn and hit the man coming across. This worked well because they moved the ball fast and the back line couldn't recover fast enough to pick the man up underneath.

One reason why Canisius's back line had a rough time was because they had trouble handling WV height.

In the second half, Canisius started looking for this play and they intercepted about four passes.

Another play:

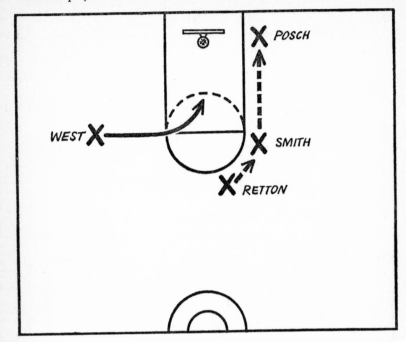

This time, Retton was the guard. Retton hit Smith. At this time West started across the key. Smith hit Posch underneath and Posch hit West. West put his left shoulder down and laid it up and in right handed.

Fast Break: They have a very good fast break. They work it two ways. (1) When the rebound is taken off they will look for the man at the top of the key and he will take the ball straight up the middle. (2) A couple of times they hit the man on the side and he hit the man in the center.

Bolyard usually leads the fast break and is terrific on it. Reminder: when on the fast break, he looks one way, then always passes the opposite way; i.e., if he looks at the man on his left, he will hit the man on his right. They also will take a chance sometimes and throw the long lead pass if the man gets behind the back guards. Canisius got caught a couple of times.

Tap Play: Only one they used:

West tapped back to Bolyard to the left of the key. Bolyard moved from the top of the key to the left.

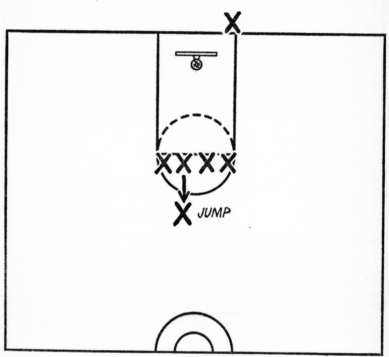

Out of bounds Play:

West sets himself second from left. He pulls straight back and takes a high pass from the man out of bounds and throws a quick jump shot. There is no attempt to block off the defensive man. They just want to catch him napping. West hit five jump shots on us on this play. All he did was back up and get the pass and hit the quick jumper.

Out of bounds Play:

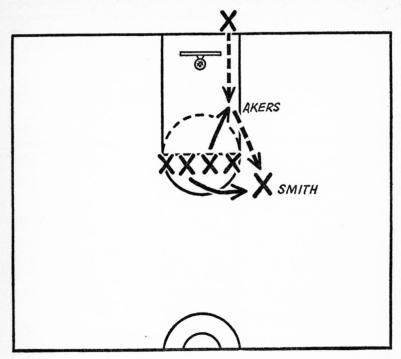

Akers second from right pulled out towards the ball and took the pass from out of bounds. Smith who was third from right pulled out towards the right sidelines and got hit with a pass from Akers and took a jump shot.

Note—Defense: On defense, they block the base line terrifically and force the man in. They keep the center blocked terrifically and force the man to drive towards the side lines. This they did to us all the time.

Another Play:

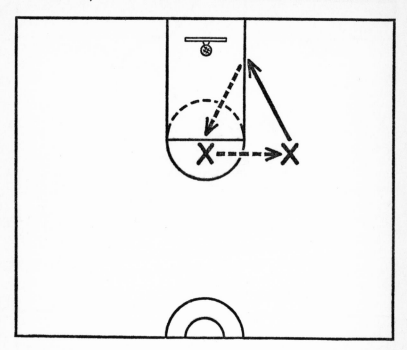

When center got the ball he would hit the man on the side. The side man would drive toward the bucket. If he got the shot he would go all the way, but if he was stopped he would hit the center. This worked two or three times. Smith worked this especially well with Clousson and Akers.

Make sure each man is picked up before he gets to the top of the key because they will dribble right up to the top of the key, stop and jump, all in one motion.

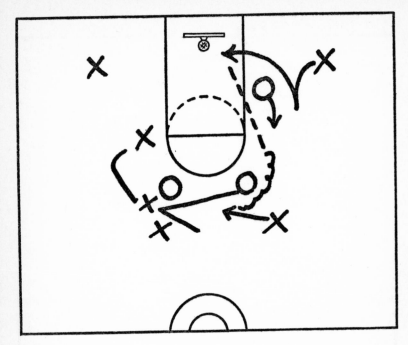

PERSONNEL:

#44 West, 6'3, 175—Tremendous! Moves very well. Terrific jump shot from anywhere. Hustles all the time. Jumps like a man 6'6. Blocked at least five or six shots. When he gets the ball around the basket he maneuvers until he gets the ball up on the boards. Puts his shoulder down and drives right in. Likes to play the left side and drives left along the base line. When he goes in on a drive he always lays the ball up with both hands. He did drive right across the key once and laid it up and in. He went right because the defensive man overplayed him to his left. I would overplay him to his left all the time because he is more dangerous that side. He is also a very good feeder and if he doesn't have the shot, he feeds. Gets down court well on the fast break.

#21 Smith, 6'4, 185—Really tough. Has tremendous hands. Could play guard or front. Very good defensively. Good jump shot. Gets down fast on the break. He likes to drive right from the right side always, looks to hit the center if his drive is stopped. He, West, Clousson and Akers hit the boards *very well*. He will lead the fast break at times. Will try to steal the ball right out of your hands. Underrated.

#30 Bolyard, 5'11, 185—Usually leads the fast break. When he looks one way he always passes the other. Shoots a two handed jump shot from the top of the key against the zone. Very good defensively. Plays the ball sometimes but if he misses it he recovers quickly. Whether he can drive or not, he didn't show—he didn't try it against the zone. Good hands— **GREAT SPEED.**

#34 Clousson, 6'6, 200—Played the key against the zone. Will turn and jump. Feeds Smith and West on the sides. Turned and hit Akers underneath quite a few times. Hits the boards hard. Will maneuver until he gets the ball upon the boards. Will hook right handed. Fair jump shot. Strong. Good control of the ball when he is shooting.

#32 Akers, 6'5, 195—Played the base line underneath against the zone defense. Leaps real well. Shots left handed hook, fair jump shot. Good off the boards. Strong. Moves well.

#25 Posch, 6'7, 205—Came in for Clousson. They are no weaker with him in their lineup. Fair jump shot, moves well and good off the boards.

#35 Ritchie, 6'5, 185—Came in for Akers. Liked this guy. He played both underneath and on the side. Good jump shot and plenty of hustle. Sets up well. Moves real well. Works hard for his shots.

#14 Retton, 5'7, 160—Came in for Bolyard. Didn't shoot much but very good defensively. Played the ball but recovered very fast when he missed it. Terrific hustle. Also very good on the fast break, but not as deceptive as Bolyard.

Summary: They are a well coached club. They surprised me defensively. They switched off very well against the zone.

On offense, they always looked to hit the center if their drive was stopped. Make sure your center always—repeat ALWAYS—has their center blocked out from the boards. *Always* keep him between the ball and his man unless naturally, the ball is out front. They all hit the boards well! They all hit the boards well!

Shaus's bench is very good, so that he substitutes freely for all but West and Smith. Watch out for Smith . . . he's a good man.

PRINCETON SCOUTING REPORT

Princeton beat Columbia 84-72 with Kaemmerlen playing his last game as he is in trouble with his studies. He means a great deal to them offensively and defensively, especially with his rebounding. But without him, Princeton still can be awfully tough, and at this time of the schedule, it would be a big mistake for any team to underrate them. They are the biggest challenger now as they are but two games back—have two games with Dartmouth—and are yet to play the other no. two club, Cornell at Princeton.

Columbia was out to stop Campbell, Ivy leading scorer, and played every one on him, but Brangan scored seven of 11 from the field while they were doing this. Both Brangan and Campbell were fouled quite often and *Campbell* had 6 for 9 from foul line, earning five field goals for 16 points, while *Brangan* had 12 for 15 from foul line and 7 field goals for *26* points. Campbell and Brangan totals were 42 points—just half of the Princeton offense. Both boys are very good foul shooters. It was *dumb* to keep fouling them out by 17' and 19'.

Kammerlen had 16 points also like two mentioned, he can shoot fouls. *Swan* likewise regarding fouls, 5 for 6, with 4 field goals for 13 points. With Kammerlen out, Brennan (6'7) probably will be replacement, and with Campbell, Brangan and Swan, Princeton would be rough all the way.

Brennan lacks experience, having played the bench last year. The fifth starter against Columbia was Burton, but he didn't play too long—about 6½ minutes—and was replaced by Higgins who went the rest of the way. Burton had 5 points, Higgins, 7 points. Cappy used these six all the way except with 2½ minutes to go in the game. Kaemmerlen—*Campbell, 6'1; Brangan, 6'1; Swan, 6'3; Higgins, 6'2*, Higgins for Burton, *Brennan 6'7;* Hyland, Whitehouse, about 2½ minutes.

In your game at Princeton, I look for the italicized players to start. Brennan scored 2 points, and Hyland and Whitehouse none.

Brangan and Campbell are very much alike as they are very good jumpers, terrific drivers and both have quick movements. Also, they thread a needle with quick passes. Split the high post clever and quick. Swan would be my #3 concern, as he can shoot and drive but not as quickly as other two players. This is a very good club against any zones as they have the jumpers. Columbia played the book against them and although on several occasions they came close, Princeton class was the answer. Oldham played man for man very tight, pressed to ½ court, full court, and used a 1-1-3 zone going into a 2-3 zone as Cappy started to sit on the ball. Princeton had Campbell, Brangan and Kammerlen inside with Swan and Higgins outside. Columbia favored Swan and gave Higgins the shot. Hell, I thought this was terrific if he had done it all the way. Zone seems to hurt Princeton and with Kammerlen out, the 1-1-3 will curtail the drivers, reduce the fouling and especially hurt them with jumpers.

Defensively, Princeton played a man to man and zone. They kept switching the defense in the first half, but in the second half, Princeton stayed to man to man.

Offensively, Princeton used 2-2-1 with the pivot man ½ way 7' to 8' and high post. This in general was the run of the game. Now to offense and defense used by Princeton.

DEFENSE: As stated, Cappon in the first half switched a great deal from man to man into zone without calling any time outs and it threw Columbia off. They used this method all thru the first half, in the second half Princeton had Columbia as Cappy stayed to a tight man to man. They both fouled very much, especially in the second half. Princeton shot 28 of 39 fouls (81 fouls). *Personals* Columbia 27, Princeton 23. Phil Fox and James Lennon. Rodin with 19 points and Needleman with 14 points led Columbia.

2-3 Zone into 2-1-2 zone.

Princeton shifted defensively with the ball across court with either 3 or 10 double teaming high post. With this 32 and 12 were getting shots but hurried shots. In fact, Princeton will dog you. Bear in mind this zone was used about every 3rd or 4th play as Columbia came down court. Columbia tried to fast break Princeton but Princeton was back all the time. In man to man, Columbia used 2-2-1, but it was all outside. Princeton used 3 and 10 defensively outside on Columbia playmakers. 30 and 23 of Princeton played side court men and 34 on the defensive post man. Brennan will probably take Kammerlen's place. Regarding switching, only the two outside men interswitched. Other three inside men stayed to man

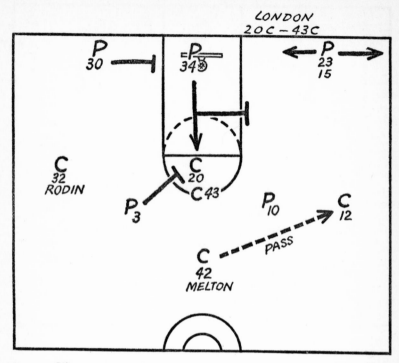

to man. These two outside men who are Princeton best will steal so your playmakers must be ready. If you give and go thru they will go with you. Columbia did not go thru enough nor did they split enough to make them switch to the post.

OFFENSE: I can not figure Columbia staying man to man as long as they did in particular in the first half. In the second half, the 1-1-3 zone into a 2-3 zone really gave Princeton trouble, as Cappy was in a 2-3 offense with Campbell and Brangan in corners, Kammerlen under and Swan and Higgins outside.

Columbia 1-1-3 Zone-vs. Princeton 2-3 Offense.

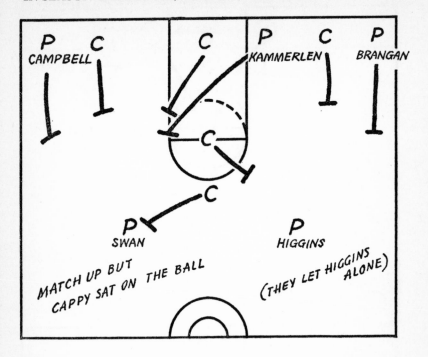

Columbia zone was too late; had they used it earlier, Princeton would have been in trouble. A box would be too hard, Doggie, as they have two very good jumpers, Campbell and Brangan.

(These four places are changed—no set positions.)

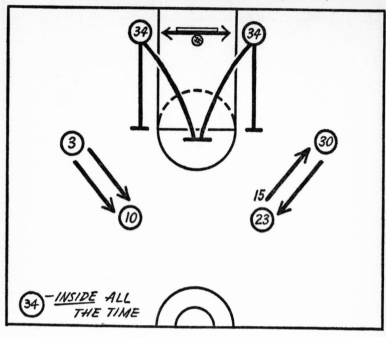

#34 Inside all the time.

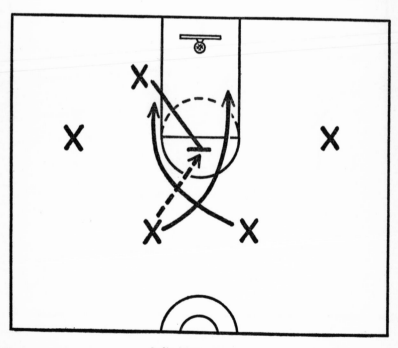

Split hit post.

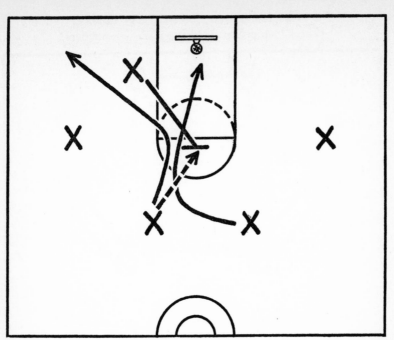

No split—both same side.

BOTH WORKED VERY GOOD.

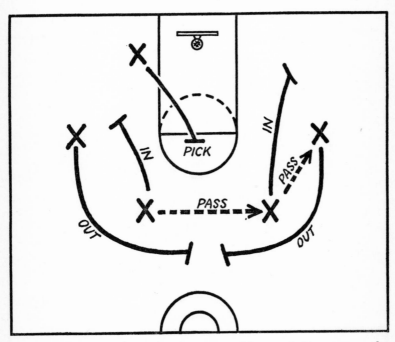

Weave in and out—change places, cause picks on their weave as they are moving.

281

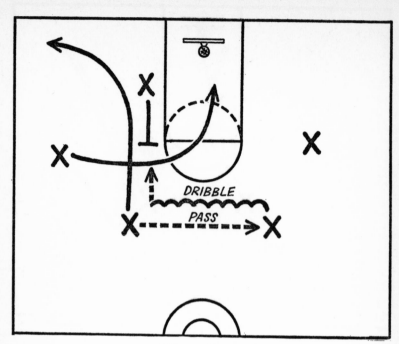

Split on side post.

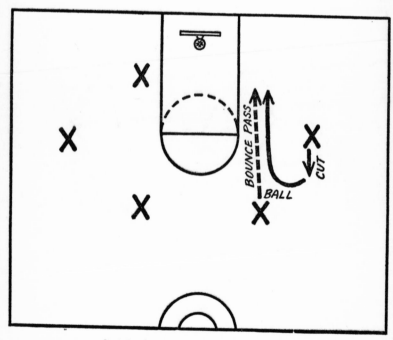

Quick play—they work it extra good.

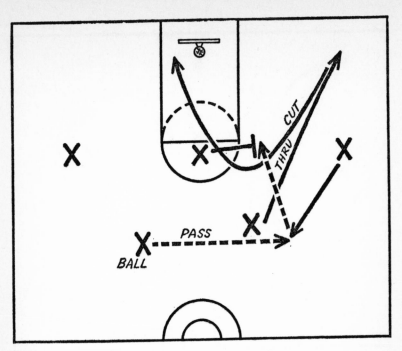

On cut goes all the way or gets jumper.

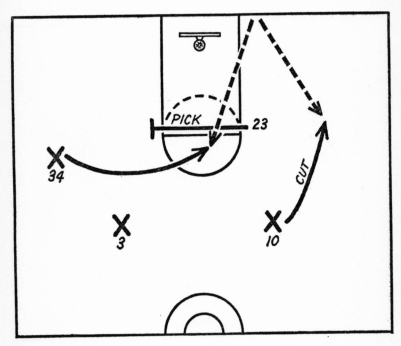

Out of bounds.

Last year I saw Cappy vs. a man to man club use a 1-2-2 with a great deal of single clearing and double clearing. Did not use against Columbia. Watch Brangan and Campbell on charge, also they drive like hell-you cause the charge.

PRINCETON PERSONNEL: They are a young ball club—only one senior, Brangan.

#3 Campbell, Soph., 6'1—16 points. Very good jumper, good driver, wears glasses. Tight defensive man. He has about 42% average. Hits on short or long jumpers. Good dribbler. Very good movements. Drive on him. A top scorer.

#10 Brangan, Sr., 6'1—26 points. Very good jumper. Very smart and good driver. Very good scorer all the way. All-Ivy last year. Will get his share of rebounds. Playing with a new group, he does a remarkable job. Very good moves. Good corner man.

#15 Burton, Jr., 6'3, 4 points. Used a good jumper. Good on the defense. Good on boards, handles ball good but Higgins is better in the over-all picture. Played first 7 minutes—then went out with three fouls.

#30 Swan, Jr., 6'3, 13 points. Good board man, good jumper, steady player. Drives very well. Handles the ball well. Will play in or out. You can not fall off him. Good hook shot.

#4 Brennan, Jr., 6'7, 2 points. Pivot man, fill in for Kammerlen. Has seen little action thus far this year. Now he should go all the way. Can hit off post. Played only 2 minutes vs. Columbia.

#23 Higgins, Jr., 6'2, 7 points. Good defensive man, good jumper. Strong under and good on tip-ins. Handled himself very well.

#11 Hyland, Jr., 5'9, No points. Very fast with a good drive. Shoots a nice jumper. Good playmaker, very good all around ball handler. Played 2 minutes.

#43 Whitehouse, Soph., 6'2—no points. Also ineligible.

THINGS THAT I THINK WILL GO: 1. Fast break. 2. Blocking out on boards and tapping out. 3. JUMP ON THEM EARLY, DON'T LET THEM RUN SHOW. 4. Make them play your game. 5. HUSTLE ON LOOSE BALLS. 6. Talk on defense and help out and when switch is made, don't let up on screener.

19

Game Procedures
and Strategy

The game procedures should be so well organized that everything works like a clock. If the coach has planned ahead and made sure his assistants, his game "chart scouts," and his managers know exactly what they are supposed to do, he will not be harassed by annoying details when he should be thinking about the game. I prepare a managers' game check list. I see that the "chart scouts" have their material and know their job of charting shots and scoring areas, assists, and opponents' offensive and defensive rebounds (as well as our own). Then I make sure my scorebook manager understands his job (checking scores with the scoreboard, the opponent's scorer and the officials), and knows how to keep me advised of the number of personal fouls (Dartmouth players as well as opponents).

GAME CHECK LIST

MANAGERS

1. Oranges and Gum
2. Boards and Baskets
3. Lights
4. Horn, Stopwatch, and Foul Paddles
5. Scoring Box (Check Clock)
6. Blackboard Charts and Chalk
7. At each bench:

285

5 Blankets

2 Buckets (One with water and cups. One with 2 wet towels and four dry towels)

1 Resin Towel

6 Practice Balls

2 Game Balls

"Heeler" Number 1

Keep time played

Watch balls at half

"Heeler" Number 2

Bench during game

When game starts take all pants and 5 jerseys to equipment room

At half-time pick up 5 jackets, oranges and gum from the equipment room

As second half starts take 5 jackets down to the equipment room.

DRESSING ROOM PROCEDURES

The dressing room atmosphere and procedures are vital factors before, during, and after the games. That may sound like a stupid and silly statement since you must dress there before the game and undress there after the game, as well as go there between the halves. But there is much more to it. Games can be won and lost here—or shall we say, a big difference can be made here in the game. I am going to break my discussion down into three parts.

1. BEFORE THE GAME. I ask my players to be completely suited-up, taped, and ready to go out on the court thirty-five minutes before game time. Part of our scouting report (players have been given a mimeographed copy) is already written on the blackboard. The most important of the report is the shot chart (opponents).

The first five minutes are spent discussing things generally and informally. If I think the players are too tense, I try to loosen them up. Perhaps a story about one of the players will do the trick. Maybe I can engage the "clown" of the team (every

HARVARD
Coached by: Floyd Wilson

3 Edward Cuffe, f   12 William Danner, f
4 Greg Loser, g   15 Robert Bowditch, f
5 Gary Borchard, f   21 Michael Donohue, g
10 Alex Hart, f   23 Bryant Danner, c
11 Marc Kolden, f   25 David Grayer, f

OFFICIALS: John Stevens, F. P. Crossin

HARVARD	Field Goals	FT	PF	TP
F 3 Cuffe	2222222222	111111	12345	
F 5 Borchard	2222222222	111111	12345	
C 23 B. Danner	2222222222	111111	12345	
G 15 Bowditch	2222222222	111111	12345	
G 21 Donohue	2222222222	111111	12345	
	2222222222	111111	12345	
	2222222222	111111	12345	
	2222222222	111111	12345	
	2222222222	111111	12345	
	2222222222	111111	12345	
	2222222222	111111	12345	

DARTMOUTH
Coached by: Alvin F. Julian

3 Bob Hoagland, g   21 Chuck Kaufman, g
4 Dave Farnsworth, c   22 Howie Keys, g
5 Gary Vandeweghe, f   23 Chuck Church, f
10 Bryant Barnes, f   24 Walt Sosnowski, g
11 Dan Berry, f   30 Bob Meyer, f
20 Bob Brower, f   42 George Ramming, c

DARTMOUTH	Field Goals	FT	PF	TP
F 10 Barnes	2222222222	11111111	12345	
F 5 Vandeweghe	2222222222	11111111	12345	
C 42 Ramming	2222222222	11111111	12345	
G 24 Sosnowski	2222222222	11111111	12345	
G 21 Kaufman	2222222222	11111111	12345	
	2222222222	11111111	12345	
	2222222222	11111111	12345	
	2222222222	11111111	12345	
	2222222222	11111111	12345	
	2222222222	11111111	12345	
	2222222222	11111111	12345	

DIAGRAM 197

287

team has one) in a little "fun" conversation. If my team does not look ready—then I get ready for a tough game. They should have gotten ready during the practices preceding the game. However, I try to point out *our* strengths as well as those of the opponents.

Perhaps you get a break because the star of the other team has not played in the last couple of games. At any rate, my first five minutes are completely informal. Under no conditions do I give the team a "pep" talk or try to stir them into a frenzy. Kids have common sense and you can talk sense to them.

One year, during a basketball game at Dartmouth, a woman turned to my wife and asked: "Is Dartmouth playing a person-to-person defense?" Well, I told my squad about the remark the next day and they got a big chuckle out of it. But it paid off later in a serious manner.

We were playing a tough game a few nights afterward and I noticed that the team was tense and tight in the dressing room. Now, I like them to be free and easy; never tense. But as I tried to take off the tension I realized that my efforts weren't clicking. The team realized it, too. Finally, "Walt" Sosnowski spoke up and said: "Coach, are we playing a person-to-person defense tonight?"

That did it! The kids howled. It broke the tension and we went out and played a helluva game and won it, too! That was timing! Real nice timing.

When I feel that they are ready, I start to talk directly about the game. We study the shot chart just to refresh our minds on the opponents' type of shooting. Then we check the shooting areas of their players. Since we know the defense we are going to use, we now make sure of every player's assignment.

The next few moments are spent in diagramming our offensive specialties for this game and reviewing them. Then I check the players for questions. The team never leaves the room without being reminded of the following:

1—"Rebound!"
2—"Take good shots!"
3—"Don't lose the ball without a good shot!"

We make sure we will be on the floor for twenty minutes

and just before going out for our pre-game work-out, we clasp hands.

There should be no confusion in a dressing room. You prepare for the games during the practices—not in the dressing room before a game.

2. BETWEEN THE HALVES: Complete relaxation without talking is the rule for the first five minutes. We need this time so the players can be checked by the trainer; can refresh themselves by eating the oranges; and can rest. However, during these first five minutes, I may talk quietly to a player concerning his individual play. But no long conversations.

At the end of the five minutes, the first half statistics are ready and I look them over and then read them to the team—good or bad! I believe in being frank with my players at all times—no equivocation!

As the time is running out, now, I hurry through the first half statistics. I read them quickly to myself and then pick out the important ones and read them to the squad. I ask each player if his opponent is making different moves from those shown on the scouting reports. If the answer is yes, we discuss the problem and make new plans which I outline on the blackboard.

I now go into our offense. I want to be sure my players are clear regarding our offense before going out for the second half. I diagram offensive plays and moves that should work against our opponent's defense.

If a change in the opponent's defense is anticipated, I try to prepare for that. A few individual instructions here and there leave me with about four minutes before the start of the second half. It is unwise to hurry. All our moves are made calmly and confidently.

3. AFTER THE GAME: I visit the dressing room before the players shower and shake hands personally with each player. Then I talk very briefly to the team and check all injuries. If we have played at home, there is no after-the-game meal problem. If we are on the road, depending on whether we play the next night, we decide whether to eat together or individually.

Do not get the idea that we are a complacent and unconcerned club when we leave the dressing room. We go out of there with plenty of life. Remember: no matter how hard you try, you cannot get your ball club up for every game. Today's athlete thinks differently from the athletes of the past. The boy today will laugh at a "pep" talk and you must be careful of the so-called "psychology" you use. Today's players will get themselves up for the big games on their own. You can talk your head off trying to get them up for the "in-between" games to no avail. But there is one thing certain—the manner in which you are trying to convey something to the boys determines the way they will react.

Bench Procedure and Strategy

Let me start out by saying that there isn't a coach in the world who knows whether a substitution he has made is going to work out good or bad until after the player has had a chance to blend with the team and the new combination has played awhile. Naturally, you hope you have made the right replacement, but how do you really know? The sub can do worse and he can do better. You are hoping for the latter.

I want our subs to feel they are part of the team at all times, and to have the right spirit with respect to "sitting the bench." Here, a sense of humor is important.

When I was with the Boston Celtics, we were playing an important game one night and I was trying to figure out the right substitution. I called Ed Leede up with the idea of putting him in the game. He kneeled down before me and then I called another player, and then another! The three of them were there in front of me and finally I put one of the other players in the game instead of Leede. Turning to the crowd, Leede raised both arms over his head and with a big grin on his face said: "Many are called but few are chosen!"

Our bench procedure is simple. Let's start with the huddle. Everyone huddles before the game starts and on every time out. Most coaches insist upon this and the reason is simple. You want every boy to know what's going on for one thing, and you want them to know they are part of the team.

We want lots of pepper from our players on the bench. We want them to be yelling encouragement to the team out there, and to be in the game every second. When we call for a substitute we want him to respond immediately and not make us ask for him two or three times. We demand that our replacements start playing the moment they get in the game. I do not believe they should be given four or five minutes to get "warmed up." After all, they practice all week with the team, they take pregame warm-ups with the team, they join the huddles, and just because they have been sitting it out for awhile is no reason they shouldn't play well when they go in. A young boy watching a game being played by his team will be "warmed up" enough just sitting there, if he has the proper spirit. I don't care if a substitute doesn't help the team, but I sure don't want him to hurt the team. So my players all know when they go in a game I expect immediate action. Maybe I'm wrong but that's what I demand.

If we get six to eight points down, unless it is very evident we are playing against an inferior team, I make a move. I will not sit there and say or hope that everything will turn out all right. Because, while I'm sitting there saying and hoping, we may get fifteen points down and then we're in real trouble.

As I said, if we get six or eight points down—I move! I'll either make a substitution, call a time-out to talk things over or change our game plays. Offense or defense. But move—I will! If that doesn't work out, and often it doesn't, I'll try something else. Another replacement, maybe, perhaps a press or semipress, or zone and combination press. I'll speed up the game or slow it down. One way or another, I'll do *something!* A coach must be like a doctor. Keep trying a different remedy till you have the right one.

I like to make substitutions on the other team's time out. Especially one where I know I'm going to put the boy back in a few minutes. Reason? Well—here I have a boy I want to give a little rest—three or four minutes at the most. I will try to take him out when the other team calls time. This gives me one minute for the boy in which there is no playing on the floor. Until play is resumed you may get another fifteen seconds. Then you rest the boy two minutes of actual playing time and finally get him back in because you can't get the clock stopped. But that can happen anytime, and meanwhile you've given your boy that extra minute and a quarter.

We like to save our time-outs until near the end of the game. If it is a close one, that is where you'll need them. If it isn't close you haven't lost anything. But I will not let our team fall too far behind or lose a game just to save a time-out. I want what I need *now*. Situations that come up later must be taken care of later. Maybe they won't happen . . . You hope!

The personality of the coach "on the bench" is important. He must maintain his poise and dignity and yet impress his players with a fighting spirit and the desire to win. It isn't easy. For example, when Dartmouth plays at Princeton, the "Tigers" bark at me (Doggie)!

I remember a professional game in Minneapolis when I was coaching the Boston Celtics. My team was having trouble with Mikan and in a moment of annoyance (Ha!) I threw my program away.

A fan yelled: "Better keep it, Doggie! You might win the radio!"

The little incident which follows required "poise" too. One night we were playing a strong opponent at home (Hanover, N.H.), and I had told the team to make certain to use a certain maneuver which I thought would pay off. My son Toby happened to be captain of that team. When the boys went back on the floor, instead of following my "strategy" directions, they did just the opposite. I called time out and said: "What's the idea? You are doing just the opposite of what I told you to do!"

Toby spoke up and said: "Well, Dad, I'll tell you how it is. . . . We thought you too could be wrong!"

Sometimes during the heat of a game the boys get a little reckless, start playing bad or crazy basketball. When I see this I can often save a time out by yelling to them and holding up three fingers (rebound, good shots, and don't lose the ball without a good shot).

With a minute or less to go before the half we are leading by five points—either we're going to come off the floor at half time with that five or maybe seven points, but never three. In other words we want that last shot. I have seen many a game lost because a team leading in the above situation insisted on taking a shot too soon, thereby enabling the other team to cut their lead to three points at the half and finally to win the game by one. Not only that, but one of your best players may have a foul called on him in the bargain. Remember, "never less than what you have but maybe two more!" We've got to have meat and potatoes with our bread and butter.

Naturally, we will change our defense or offense anytime we think it will help. We do not always wait until we are behind to press. We may press when we are ahead if we think it will help. One thing we try to do—never let our opponents play like they have practiced. Of course, we aren't always successful in doing this.

We don't always press when we're behind, near the end of the game. Sometimes the team who is five (5) ahead with three minutes to go isn't satisfied to beat us only by five. They want to win by twenty (20). So they keep shooting. Here, we will not press. We played a game with a college I won't mention. With 3:40 left, they were leading by seven points. I didn't order the press.

My assistant said: "Doggie, we've got to put on the press." I said: "No, this team isn't satisfied to win by seven. They want to beat us by twenty!"

Well, they kept shooting and we beat them by one. Usually, however, the opposite is the case.

If I were eight down with five minutes to go and had just been swapping baskets and made no gain on them—then I'd press. Say we're one down with forty seconds to go and the other team is freezing. We want that ball and it looks like we must foul to get it. We will not foul at once but will wait for about fifteen seconds hoping they will make a mistake or we can steal the ball. If that is not successful, we will foul and hope they will miss the free-throw. We feel we still have enough time to win.

Today, with the new foul rules, play is governed quite a bit. Are you in the one-and-one or just one-foul category? If you are five points ahead with about one minute to go and you are not in the one-and-one foul rule situation, you should foul at once (even though you are ahead). That way your opponents can gain only one point. But you have the ball and now that is what you want. They must come and get it! In that situation, don't let them score the field goal.

If you are three points ahead with ten seconds to go, just stand there on defense. No three-point play! Even if they score a field goal leaving you only one ahead you still have five seconds to bring the ball in from out-of-bounds and ten seconds in the back court. By then the game will be over and you don't need to bring it up.

If we're in a good, tight game, say leading by four points but can't seem to get the next one to put us six up, we will call "time" and use what we call a "clutch play." We want that next bucket, that next two points, to try to break the game open. Of course, we'll do this right before the half, too, when the score is tied.

Say we are eight points ahead with three or four minutes to play and are using our semi-freeze offense. Here, we'll try to score only if we have a real "Gussie" (with no one near us). If we are putting on the freeze with a one, two, or three point lead and with a minute or two to go, we do not try to score unless our opponents force us to shoot. In the case of a tie, we'll hold the ball and try for the "last shot," even if it means holding the ball as long as two or three minutes. Either we're going to win or we go into overtime. But we won't take the chance of losing. . . .

However, a lot of things you do depend on your personnel and the personnel of your opponent. Can your players handle the ball well enough to freeze it? Can they press? Do they have speed? Can they make their free throws? Can they stand up under pressure? Do we have a good dribbler?

Of course, the same questions must be applied to your opponent. Your strategy will depend a great deal on the answers to these questions.

In a good tight game you should know which one of your opponent's players to foul (the poorest shooter). Which one of your players should do the fouling (the one who has the least number of personal fouls).

Save that best play you have to get the two points you need. Don't *always* set up your high scorer. Go with someone else once in a while. Try to have a piece of paper in your pocket on which you can diagram the play you want set up. Then show it to the players and tell each one his exact position. They can then remember it better, even though they may have practiced the play until they have it down pat.

Once we were playing Villanova in Philadelphia and were ahead in the score with fifteen minutes to go. In a time-out huddle I said: "We're fifteen minutes from Madison Square Garden." Later, with sixty seconds to go we were ahead by five. Villanova took a time out and one of my boys said: "We're only sixty seconds from Broadway, Coach!"

There are five seconds to go. You are leading by three or more points and the opponents have the ball. Here, the risk of a foul is too much to take. It is better to let the opponents drive and make the basket than to attempt to defend against the score. "Give them two points and get the ball!"

Once we were playing a team that was supposed to beat us badly. At the end of the first five minutes we were ahead by ten points. The opponents called time out. My players came to the bench and huddled around me. I let them get their breath and get sponged off but said nothing. It was almost time to resume play and one of the boys said: "Coach, aren't you going to tell us anything?"

I said: "Fellows, you're ahead by ten. Anything I say can only hurt you. Just keep doing what you *are* doing."

I bring this point up because a lot of coaches think that they must say something every time there is a time out. Sometimes there is no need. Save your advice until it's needed—and then say it!

The above is pertinent to the following situation. You are

leading by twenty in the second half and are playing a certain type of ball. Now, you tell your club to be careful, slow it down and take fewer and also better shots. Next thing you know, you aren't doing so well and the other team starts to catch up. When you are going good, leave well enough alone. You can't do any better than win. . . .

However, if we are ahead by four near the end of the game, we don't have to win by six. . . . That is what beats a lot of teams. Never mind the national ratings or the high-scoring race. "That's for Sweeny!"

20

Preparation for Tournament Play

In preparing for a tournament, much depends on the time remaining between the last game of the season and the first game of the tournament. If it is anywhere from ten days to two weeks, we usually give the team three entire days off from practice. Then I practice every other day for about a week and then every day for the last three or four days.

You must keep in mind that you are at the tail end of the season and that practices must not be long, drawn-out affairs. They must be short and to the point! If you know who your first opponent is going to be, most of the time should be spent preparing an offense and defense for that opponent. Knowing what other teams will be in the tournament will give you a chance to make plans in general which may be used in the tournament.

One thing I stress in preparing for tournament play is defense. I work on the assumption that the team may have the jitters or may have a cold shooting night. That is where defense will come in handy. As stated earlier in this book, the year my Holy Cross team won the NCAA, I stressed defense in preparation for the tournament and the result was that none of our opponents scored fifty points against us. We were behind in each of the three games at the beginning and pulled them all out, and I attributed the victories to the fact that while we were cold we were playing fine defensive ball.

297

The scouting report on the first team you are to play will always be better than those of succeeding games. You never know your second opponent until after the results of the first round. Because of this we have several men watch the games of the "possible" second-round opponents. Here, we stress shot charts. We want particularly to know from what areas their shooters can hit. Next, I want to know what attack they worked best against their opponent's defenses. What was their reaction to the press? To a zone as compared to the man-to-man defense? What defenses do they use? Are they aggressive?

Naturally, the above is only a part of the scouting report, but here time is of the essence and it is folly to load your team up with too many points concerning the next opponents. "Let the other team worry about us!"

Many coaches may not agree, but I think it is wise to start tournament talk at the beginning of the season. I start talking to the team about getting into a tournament almost from the first practice and keep hammering at them to have a good year and to win the league so we will get into tournament play. I feel that most players regard tournament play as a reward for a good season.

Again, in getting ready for the tournament games I try to stop all practices at the peak rather than overdo them.

I want my team to be tournament hungry and I am constantly on the lookout for the ball players who have been only substitutes during the season. Many times they will come up with great tournament play. You have to use them to find out if they are ready. You go for broke in a tournament and you must pull out all the stops! There is no tomorrow.

Except for the fact that you have to keep in mind the overall picture of the tournament, I would say that tournament preparation is not too different from getting ready for an important league game. In a short tournament series it is wise to prepare your team for things which the other teams in the tournament do not expect—a change of defensive or offensive alignment may be all that is needed to upset a strong opponent. You go all out! This is it! You will gamble more in a tournament than you will in the league season and you expect that 101 per cent effort from your players.

TRAVEL PLANS

Your travel plans should be all prepared several days in advance of the trip, so the players may tell their parents and friends when they are leaving and when they will arrive at the tournament site. If you can determine the name of the hotel or other quarters where you will be housed it is a good item to tell the players.

ARRIVAL

We usually try to get to the site of the tournament two days ahead of time, so that the boys will have a chance to get used to the general atmosphere of the hotel or other living quarters and to get generally acquainted with the atmosphere of the town or city.

EATING AND SLEEPING

We like the players to eat together and to follow as closely as possible their regular "at home" diet. The same applies to sleeping habits and rest. While I feel that the players should have a little fun, I impress them with the point that the trip has been for one purpose—to win the tournament! After we have won, we'll have some fun!

MANAGER RESPONSIBILITIES

Our managers have the responsibility, along with the trainer, of making sure we have the right equipment, that we know the suit colors of our possible opponents, that we will have two or three sets of uniforms in case we should meet "suit color" difficulties, etc. We use our regular Managers' Check Lists to insure that all necessary items will be covered.

PRACTICES

I want my players to get acquainted with the floor, the lights, the baskets and the distance behind them, the crowds and the general feel of the gymnasium or field house. I think it is wise to watch (when possible) the work-outs of other teams as well as tournament games which are played at any time except just previous to OUR game. Get your players used to all the excitement and noises, colors, cheers and boos, work of officials, timers, scorers, clocks, and anything and everything which might distract them during the BIG game (the one *they* play).

WARM-UP

I like plenty of time to warm-up. Track men have the right idea. They work and work until they are just right. I realize there is a big difference in the amount of time each sport involves but I want my players warmed-up when the game *starts*—not at the end of the first quarter.

MEETINGS

I like to have several pre-game meetings so I can get the players mentally prepared for our final talk. I want them to be prepared emotionally as well as physically. I think it is important right here to make sure that you don't worry your team about the other team. I like to have my boys feel that the opponents should be worrying about us. Heck! we've got a lot of tricks up our sleeves and they can't possibly know what we might pull. . . .

DRAW SHEET

I like to discuss the draw sheet with the players, analyzing, to the best of my ability, attacks and defenses of the other teams, their players, etc. But I concentrate on our first opponent. "You've got to win 'em one at a time!"

ENTERTAINMENT

It is important to keep the players' thoughts off the "big" game, but I don't want them to think that they came all the way up or down here to be entertained. Entertainment is fine but we sure didn't come here to "do the town" or "see the sights!"

On the Job

It is imperative that the coach stay with his players. He shouldn't get tied up with speeches, luncheons, radio and television appearances, shows, sportswriters and photographers, and/or friends, fans, and other coaches. Some coaches do this to the extent that they forget they haven't yet won the tournament.

Publicity

Be frank with the press! Don't alibi or play down your team. Be modest but confident and make it clear that you have faith in your players. The kids will like that! They depend upon you for leadership and if you want them to believe in you—believe in them!

Pre-Game Procedures

Now, when you're getting close to game time, proceed as usual. Don't vary a thing in your pre-game procedure. Make it just like home. Keep the fans and friends and the fathers and the mothers and other well-wishers out of the dressing room. Be calm personally. Set the example. Act as you always do. Don't pace back and forth with a worried frown on your face as if the fate of the world rests on your broad shoulders. Be businesslike and confident and SMILE once in a while. How can you eliminate player-tension when every move *you make* "spells the word?"

NO TURMOIL! NO FEVER OF PREPARATION!
NO HURRY UP AND WAIT!
CALM CONFIDENCE IS THE PROPER ATTITUDE

Win or Lose

Of course, the big let-down will come if you are eliminated in the first game. If you lose, stick with your players like glue.

You're all together and, trite as it may sound, it's "One for all and all for one!" If you win, give the credit to the players. Agree with all the fans and friends and Dads and Moms. . . . "You're right! Pete's the greatest! What a game! And how about Jimmy? And little ole Red! And, Marty! And Bill and Murph and Skinny and Fats and—hey! How about the manager? Did you see how quick he got the first aid case out there when Murph had the nose bleed? What a gang!"

CONSOLATION GAME

It's hard to get your team up for a consolation game, but there's a big word in the Dartmouth basketball dictionary and it goes right along with winning or losing. It's PRIDE! We fight with all we've got to win *every* contest—practice game or championship game!

TOURNAMENT HUNGRY

That just about wraps it up as far as tournament preparation goes. . . . Naturally, we try to get movies and a good scouting report on the other teams, but we don't stop there. We make sure we are ready for anything. Now, one last word. Inferior teams win championship tournaments every year, simply because they were tournament hungry and played "bread and butter basketball!"